JB JOSSEY-BASS

LOGIC MODELING METHODS IN PROGRAM EVALUATION

Joy A. Frechtling

BICENTENNIAL
1807
WILEY
2007
BICENTENNIAL

John Wiley & Sons, Inc.

Published by Jossey-Bass
A Wiley Imprint
989 Market Street, San Francisco, CA 94103-1741   www.josseybass.com

Library of Congress Cataloging-in-Publication Data

Frechtling, Joy A.
  Logic modeling methods in program evaluation / Joy Frechtling.
      p. cm.
  Includes bibliographical references and index.
  ISBN 978-0-7879-8196-9 (cloth)
  1. Evaluation—Methodology. 1. Title.
  AZ191.F74 2007
  001.4—dc22

                                        2007002844

Printed in the United States of America

FIRST EDITION
PB Printing 10 9 8 7 6 5 4 3 2 1

Contents

List of Figures

To my husband, Doug, and my son, Dan

PREFACE

This book introduces a range of audiences to an immensely useful tool called the *logic model* and the related process of *logic modeling*. As you proceed through the chapters in this volume, you will be introduced to this tool and learn how to use it. Before delving into the individual chapters, we outline the purpose of this book and the types of users it can serve.

Logic Modeling Methods in Program Evaluation shows readers how the logic model can inform the evaluation of projects ranging from small to large and from simple to complex. More reference than step-by-step guide, the book nonetheless outlines the steps for developing, using, and revising the tool to promote more useful and relevant evaluations. With this goal in mind, we discuss not only the strengths of using a logic model but also the challenges in using it effectively. As with many potentially useful tools, it is possible to misuse the logic model or use it in inappropriate ways.

The primary audience for this book is evaluators, both new learners and more experienced practitioners who want to learn more about the approach. Although logic models to date have been most popular in education, health, and community change efforts, this tool can be applied to almost any field in which evaluation occurs. Logic modeling, however, is not compatible with all types of evaluation: some methodologies and evaluation belief systems rest on assumptions that do not mesh well with the assumptions underlying this tool.

A secondary audience comprises policymakers, funders, and program managers who work with evaluators. These groups can benefit from understanding the logic model even if they are not direct implementers of the evaluation process. Further, because we have seen that the logic model can apply to activities beyond the evaluation phase, we believe that this broader stakeholder group will find additional uses for the approach. The logic model can be used in many ways for strategic planning, team building, or program design.

Finally, it is important to understand that this book is written with practical utility squarely in mind. Although the theoretical underpinnings of the logic model are addressed, the main purpose of this book is to describe and explain how the model can be used, not to ground the approach in evaluation theory. Thus we draw on many examples from our own evaluation work, some of which we consider exemplary, others of which are better described as amusing.

Acknowledgments

Work on this book benefited greatly from the support and guidance of Andy Pasternack and Seth Schwartz at Jossey-Bass. I also want to gratefully thank my colleagues at Westat—Xiaodong Zhang, Brian Kliener, and Gary Silverstein—for allowing me to use their work as illustrations in the book. A final thanks goes to Amber Winkler, another Westat colleague, whose work with me in the development of a range of evaluation workshops has clearly influenced the content of this book.

About the Author

Joy A. Frechtling is a vice president and associate director in Westat's Education Studies Group. She has more than thirty years' experience conducting educational evaluation, addressing all levels of the educational system. She has worked in a variety of research areas, including early literacy, mathematics and science education, educational reform, assessment, and professional development. She is a member of the American Evaluation Association and the American Educational Research Association, for which she served as secretary and vice president for Division H, School Evaluation and Program Development. She has a Ph.D. in developmental psychology from George Washington University.

CHAPTER ONE

EVALUATION AND LOGIC MODELS

The logic model has become a powerful and useful tool for *scaffolding* evaluations, helping to define and clarify what should be measured and when. In this first chapter, we present background information intended to situate logic modeling within current and complementary analytic trends. The chapter:

- Introduces the idea of a logic model
- Discusses program evaluation and how the logic model supports evaluation
- Highlights the contribution of *program theory*
- Shows how logic modeling relates to both the *systems approach* and *performance management*

The objective of this discussion is to place logic modeling within the context of a broader range of strategies for information gathering and generation, and lay out the assumptions or biases on which the remainder of the book rests.

THE LOGIC MODEL

What is a logic model? Basically, it is a tool that describes the *theory of change* underlying an intervention, product, or policy. It characterizes a project through a system of elements that include components and connections, with context being an important qualification. Although this book addresses the use of logic modeling for evaluation, the logic model actually has a much wider range

1

of applications. It can be used as a tool for planning, for managing, or for documenting innumerable activities from educational intervention to organizational redesign and problem solving.

Recently, the logic model has become a popular tool in evaluation circles. The Kellogg Foundation has been recognized as a prime advocate and disseminator of the logic model (see *Using Logic Models to Bring Together Planning, Evaluation, and Action: Logic Model Guide*, published in 2000). Federal agencies too, such as the Department of Education, the Centers for Disease Control, and the National Science Foundation, have all promoted use of logic models in the evaluation process.

Logic modeling is a tool and an approach for depicting the critical elements in a project and identifying where evaluation is most important. It is a tool used by people and with people; thus it takes skill and practice in employing the types of thinking and negotiating that must be done.

Although logic modeling has its own "rules of operation," results differ widely depending on whether these rules are applied thoughtfully or mechanically. When real thought and engagement are involved, the results can be very informative, even transformative. If applied mechanically, the payoff can be reduced to virtually zero.

In Chapter Three, we begin a close examination of the logic model and how it is developed and applied to evaluation projects. In this chapter, we look more closely at what is meant by evaluation and how the logic model fits into contemporary evaluation thinking.

WHAT EVALUATION IS ABOUT

There are many theories of evaluation and approaches to collecting evaluation information. Stufflebeam (2001) identifies twenty-two approaches to evaluation, some more "laudatory" than others. Evaluations can differ on many dimensions, among them design (experimental, quasi-experimental, regression discontinuity, and so on), intent (advocacy versus objective assessment), philosophical underpinnings (quantitative versus qualitative), and others. Evaluation is not a process or an approach; it is a family of activities.

This book does not make any presumptions about what evaluation is, but rather only about what evaluation is intended to do. We start with the assumption that the purpose of evaluation is to yield information about how well an intervention, product, or system is working. Evaluation includes description, but by its very nature evaluation cannot stop there. It looks at what is happening, in various ways and through various lenses, and assesses the value of what is found. "Objectivity" is frequently a criterion for sound, unbiased evaluation, but assessing, valuing, interpreting, and engaging the stakeholder community—all activities that involve judgment—are the essential components of the evaluation enterprise.

We also start with the assumption that evaluation is more than a judgment of ultimate success or failure. This was frequently the approach taken in evaluations of major government programs initiated in 1960 that focused primarily on the question of did it work or didn't it?—or in more traditional evaluation efforts that focus solely on what has been called "summative evaluation." Instead we believe that evaluation should be designed to inform improvement or modification both in the future and as a project is unfolding. This *formative evaluation* role, which acknowledges the importance of looking at both implementation and progress, has become increasingly important over time.

Our proposed definition of evaluation—offering a judgment of what is happening and including both formative and summative elements—leads to two additional characteristics of the evaluation process: it should be an integral part of an activity from the beginning, and it must rest on a thorough understanding of what a particular project is about. Let's explore these two ideas.

First, because many people felt that evaluation was intended to address only the question of whether or not a particular goal was achieved, too frequently evaluation began near, or even at, the end of a project. Most evaluators today recount endless stories of desperate grantees or program managers contacting them with the plea, "My project ends in two months and I have to have an evaluation. Can you help me?" However, increasing use of evaluation as a tool for program improvement, a tool for ongoing and midcourse correction, has led to recognition that evaluation needs to be part of a project from the beginning, with the most astute including an evaluator in the planning phase. Figure 1.1 shows the program planning evaluation cycle. As can be seen, evaluation is really a process that begins at the planning stage and continues to feed into the project at each subsequent stage of implementation. The power of including what might be called *evaluation thinking* at the beginning of a planning effort is increasingly recognized by program developers and state policy makers.

Including the evaluator early on helps to increase the chances that you can, in fact, answer the questions you wish to address, that appropriate measures for assessing critical variables of interest can be found or developed, and that you will be able to obtain early status or *baseline data*—data on what is happening before your project begins—in areas in which you hope to see an impact. This issue of obtaining baseline data is critically important. Unless what you are studying is routinely captured through historical records, it is almost impossible to recreate baseline measures after a study has begun. Further, the form in which the data are kept in such records may not be the form you need for addressing your questions.

Second, in a purely outcome-focused evaluation it is possible for an evaluator to assess attainment of goals without having any idea of how the project went about trying to reach those goals. If all you want to know is whether or not a *treatment* reduced the likelihood of a student dropping out of school, it is sufficient, given the appropriate evaluation design, to have measures of dropouts before and after the intervention and to compare changes against

FIGURE 1.1. THE ROLE OF EVALUATION THINKING.

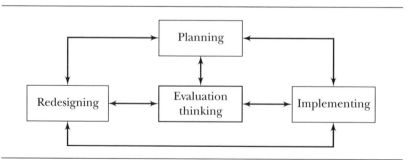

some standard or control group. However, evaluators who conduct formative evaluation are expected to know and understand in some detail what a project is about and the assumptions or theory that underlies it. To conduct a successful formative evaluation and produce information for improvement, the underlying logic of an intervention or reform must be adequately understood. When evaluating a drop-put prevention program, the evaluator needs to know the critical features of the intervention process, the length of time it was expected to occur, the expectations for student participation and engagement, and so on. In the vast majority of evaluations, the job of the evaluator is to look carefully at what is supposed to happen, measure what does happen, and highlight any deviations requiring attention or raising concern.

Returning to our definition of evaluation (the purpose of evaluation is to produce information about how well an intervention, product, or system is working), we find that this means bringing an objective, educated eye to the project as it develops, from project initiation to project conclusion. Evaluation, then, is not an event but a process. The logic model is a tool for helping to shape evaluation across the stages of evolution of a project. It reflects formative issues as well as summative. As we discuss in the chapters that follow, the logic model can support addressing the many questions that arise as a project matures.

LOGIC MODELS AND EVALUATION THEORY

It is the contention of this book that the logic model can be used with a great variety of evaluation theories or approaches. McLaughlin and Jordan (2004) talk about a logic model as an advance organizer for conducting (an implementation) evaluation. However, historically, the logic model is most closely associated with an approach called "program theory." Program theory offers a way of making explicit the assumptions underlying an intervention. It describes the causal linkages that are assumed to occur from project start to goal attainment and clearly defines the theory of change underlying a program or policy. Program theory is best described as an approach to thinking about evaluation, not a specific method of evaluation. It offers a structure onto which a variety of methodologies can be mapped (Connell and Kubisch, 1998).

Carol Weiss (1997) has chronicled the evolution of program theory, taking it back to its roots in the 1960s. According to Weiss, program theory did not become visible until the 1980s. Even then, published studies were limited. Joseph Wholey spurred increased interest in application of program theory in his work on "evaluability assessment" (Wholey, 1979, 1983), which highlighted the importance of having an adequately articulated program before evaluation should be undertaken. Program theory as a basis for evaluation crossed the line into popularity in the mid-1990s, when Weiss applied it to community-based programs (Weiss, 1995) and Wholey showed how it complimented and supported the federal government's new accountability effort, the *Government Performance and Results Act,* or GPRA (Wholey, 1997). Since then, use of program theory as a basis for evaluation has increased, as has debate over its strengths and weaknesses.

Callow-Heusser, Chapman, and Torres define it this way: "Program Theory—The set of assumptions about the manner in which the program relates to the social benefits it is expected to produce, and the *strategy* and tactics the program has adopted to achieve its goals and objectives" (2005, p. 38).

It is important to recognize that in program theory "theory-driven" does not mean that the presumed strategy is necessarily derived from a research base. Research-driven theory is entirely possible, but it is also likely (and acceptable) to have program theories that are based on practitioner experience. Thus theories of how to facilitate community engagement in disease prevention, motivate people to participate in a clinical trial, or implement a new curriculum can legitimately be developed from practitioners' experience in carrying out similar programs or from a series of research studies.

Regardless of the type of theory underlying a particular intervention or change approach, the key is defining the components of an activity or intervention and making the connections between them explicit—what the pieces are and how they work. Program theory places special emphasis on spelling out the steps that should occur and detailing intermediate processes.

Program theory evaluation (PTE) is a kind of evaluation guided by, and focused on, assessing the underlying theory of change. According to Rogers, Petrosino, Huebner, and Hacsi (2000), "PTE consists of an explicit theory or model of how the program causes the intended or observed outcomes." (p. 5).

Further, according to Weiss (2000) PTE helps to specific not only the *what* of program outcomes but also the *how* and *why*. By assessing whether expected connections occur and intermediate steps emerge, the evaluator is in essence trying to assess the validity of the explanatory mechanisms that have been posited. Where reality diverges from theory, new explanations must be developed to account for what was observed; this may result in tweaking the theory, or in the extreme dismantling it. In evaluation based on program theory, formative evaluation takes on special importance, because it is the formative evaluation component that addresses whether or not the expected intermediate steps are observed and confirmed. Let's consider an example.

Professional development for teachers has long been a popular strategy among those seeking to improve and reform public education. Professional development for teachers receives resource support from a range of federal and private funding sources, and myriad evaluations have attempted to assess the relationship between professional development and student learning. Although what works with regard to professional development is an area of much debate, a cornerstone of the legislation driving education during the first decade of the twenty-first century is provision of content-focused professional development. Standards-based, content-focused professional development is deemed to be critical, according to data showing that teachers—especially those in urban and rural environments—lack deep understanding of core subject matter. Deficits are especially severe for middle school science. Remedies to address this problem can take many forms and formats. Central, however, is the requirement that they be of extended duration and that disciplinary faculty from institutions of higher education play a significant role. Programs are seen as successful when student achievement, as measured by tests that are aligned to content standards, meets or exceeds an established standard of proficiency.

The theory of change underlying this program could be depicted simply as

Professional development	→	Teacher knowledge	→	Learning

However, such a depiction would be a theory in only the grossest sense; the three terms can mean so many things. Looking back on the initial description of what the legislation requires, one sees clearly that these terms should be further defined to accurately reflect the program theory.

Evaluation of this theory or model would need to include careful formative evaluation, of both implementation and progress, in addition to assessing whether or not test performance increased. Implementation evaluation would examine whether or not the professional development was in fact extended over time (however that term is defined) and whether or not the engagement of faculty was carried out as planned. Progress evaluation would assess the degree to which teachers did in fact have increases in their content knowledge. Finally, summative assessment would examine changes in proficiency test performance. The PTE evaluation would not be adequate or complete unless each piece and its connections were examined.

Weiss (1997, 2000) suggests that program theory can substitute for classical experimental study using random assignment. She suggests that if predicted steps between an activity and an outcome can be confirmed in implementation, this matching of "theory" to outcomes will lend a strong argument for "causality": "If the evaluation can show a series of micro-steps that lead from inputs to outcomes, then causal attribution *for all practical purposes* seems to be within reach" (1997, p. 43).

Cook (2000) takes exception to this contention, pointing out that frequently multiple theories could underlie any one relationship and that program theory does not typically permit comparative assessment of their accuracy. He suggests that instead of seeing program theory as an alternative to true experiments, program theory should be used in conjunction with true experiments to enhance the value of a study.

THE LOGIC MODEL, SYSTEMS THEORY, AND PERFORMANCE MEASUREMENT

Logic modeling has also been shaped by an area of thought called "systems theory" and "performance management."

According to Leonard and Beer (1994), "Adapting a systems approach means putting the emphasis on the big picture or the whole and considering the functions of a system's parts based on their relations with one another and within the system's larger context" (p. 1). The type of evaluative situation in which a logic model can be most effective is precisely the one systems theory has been designed to address. Such situations are characterized by rapid change, multiple interests, limited resources, and high complexity; and causality that is not linear but rather with multiple feedback loops and circular interactions.

The systems approach also recognizes that multiple lenses can be brought to an activity or phenomenon; instead of assuming one perspective or one focus, the assumption is that there are systems nested within systems. At any one time, macro or micro analyses may be relevant. As we shall see, there are frequently logic models within logic models, such that where to zoom in and zoom out becomes a strategic decision.

Finally, systems theory recognizes that change is not a confounding factor but an intrinsic feature. It is a given that phenomena are dynamic and not static. The assumption "other things being equal" does not apply. There is acknowledgment that the system must continue to function and adapt as its parts evolve, the environment changes, and relationships change.

One feature of systems theory that may or may not sit well with some evaluators is the notion that context is extremely important. What is true in one context may spectacularly fail to be true in another. Those who place high value on broad generalizability of findings and see external validity as critical to successful evaluation may feel this feature invalidates this approach; those who have struggled with findings that continue to show differential effectiveness across different contexts may feel themselves validated.

Performance management brings another set of concerns and emphases that also are found in evaluation using logic models.

Along with reliance on an underlying theory of change such as that described by Wholey (1997), performance management, like logic models, stresses the importance of identifying accurate *indicators* of change at critical junctures. As stated by Uusikyla and Valovirta (2004), a significant problem in performance management is that the indicators used may be opportunistic and not reflective of "the underlying logic with which societal changes are to be generated" (p. 2). In later chapters, we discuss the important role of the logic model in scaffolding the evaluation design and helping evaluators identify the indicators of change that are most relevant to testing whether or not the program logic is confirmed.

SUMMARY

In this opening chapter, we have discussed how the logic model fits with other approaches to and theories of assessment. First we have looked at evaluation writ large, emphasizing the importance of conceiving evaluation as both a formative and a summative endeavor. Second, we have linked logic modeling to program theory, showing how both emphasize the need for, and power of, a coherent theory of change, involving components and connections. Finally, we have shown how systems theory and performance management relate to logic modeling, the first because of its assumption of the importance of understanding the whole and the context in which it is evolving, and the latter because of the emphasis placed on identifying performance indicators that truly reflect the underlying theory of change.

QUESTIONS TO CONSIDER

1. Suggest an intervention and develop alternative theoretical explanations for what is expected to occur.
2. Discuss the term *evaluation thinking* and what it might mean.
3. What is meant by the statement that "evaluation is a process, not an event?"
4. Consider the statement that the purpose of evaluation is to generate information about how well an intervention, product, or system is working. Do you agree or disagree with this statement? Why?

CHAPTER TWO

THE USES OF LOGIC MODELS

The focus of this book is on how logic models can be used to support evaluation. However, logic models can also be used in many other ways. In this chapter, we talk about how a logic model can be useful. Several interrelated uses are described:

- Clarifying what is really intended in a project or policy
- Enhancing communication among project team members
- Managing the project
- Designing an evaluation plan and determining the questions to be addressed
- Documenting a project and how it worked
- Examining a program or constellation of projects

Those involved in a project often develop plans that yield a skeletal framework that falls short on details. The saying that the devil is in the details is never so true as in a project based on a good idea that somehow doesn't work.

Why does this happen? In some cases, it is because the developers know each other and what they want to do so well that they speak in shorthand, assuming a shared understanding of what the shorthand means in operational terms. In other cases, haste, failure to adequately examine the research base, or not understanding the challenges that may be faced result in a plan that is simply not well thought out. For a variety of reasons, designs are frequently poorly specified, and when problems arise it is too late or costly to make changes. Here we discuss two typical problems. One we call the *silo effect*, a situation in which the parts of a project are assumed to be interrelated but in reality stand alone.

The second we call "not knowing where you are going," or not having shared definitions for what it means to achieve success.

First, the silo effect. This occurs when the pieces of a project are thought about independently without really considering whether they fit any real theory of change. Project developers have a set of activities they want to carry out and a set of goals they want to achieve, and they assume there will be a connection. Unfortunately, the connection does not appear. Why does this happen? In some cases, activities are selected on the basis of what planners know how to do or have already started to do without careful analysis of whether or not they should be expected to lead to the desired results. In other cases, faddish activities are undertaken because of their currency rather than their appropriateness. At best, such activities may be irrelevant; at worst, they may be disruptive.

For example, a project wanting to encourage undergraduate students to become teachers identified as the key activity development of portfolios by the students engaged in some form of student teaching. Portfolios or journals are a popular tool for capturing student thought and, hopefully, leading students to think more deeply about the activities in which they have been engaged. Portfolios, it is believed, would make students more reflective about their teaching experiences and constitute a basis for discussion among communities of learners. However, in this instance little attention was given to other aspects of the student teaching experience, assuming a business-as-usual approach. When a logic model was developed and questions raised about the underlying theory of change, all agreed that simply developing a portfolio was unlikely to promote an interest in teaching without additional supports. The missing pieces were easily identified. The team still felt that the activity—developing portfolios—had some merit as a tool for enhancing the education of potential teachers, but on reflection the team did not see it as powerful enough, in and of itself, to change the number or quality of those selecting the profession. Once a logic model was developed and connections between activities and expected outcomes were more closely examined, it became clear that the design was incomplete and that additional activities had to be included.

A second frequent problem is lack of clear definition of critical outcome variables. The outcomes may be defined at a conceptual level, without adequate attention being paid to what the particular construct means in concrete terms and what level of attainment qualifies as a success. The outcome variable has not been adequately operationalized, with the result that team members hold differing definitions of what is expected to be accomplished. Even with an outcome as apparently clear as "student learning," it is not uncommon for project developers to fail to specify what is meant by this term. Potential rival definitions could include a change in performance on a high-stakes test, grades, course enrollments, or classroom behaviors—and variations in how much change is expected to occur. Unpleasant surprises can occur when one set of partners is willing to accept test performance and another feels that test performance is only a superficial indicator of genuine learning. For terms that are still less clearly defined (such as "enhanced collaboration"), problems are even more likely and troublesome.

Developing a logic model at the design stage, before efforts are misdirected or investments are incorrectly made, can be extremely useful in clarifying where pieces are not appropriately connected or terms do not have shared definitions. As a first step, the partners should clearly map the expected connections between activities and outcomes and define the intermediate steps that link the two. Using research or practitioner knowledge to support the predicted linkages is important. A second step requires operationalizing the outcome variables and agreeing on a definition of success. It is useful to brainstorm what the alternative definitions might be and systematically determine which ones might be accepted and which are out of bounds (because they do not fit assumed meanings, cannot be attained in the time that is available, or are not measurable). These discussions can have iterative effects, with clarification of outcomes leading to reexamination of activities and their adequacy.

Developing a logic model early on can have significant long-term benefits. But the activity also can have a downside. Logic model development can be a long process, and reaching agreement may slow down the rest of the work that needs to be done. The activity can be especially frustrating when choices lead to reconsideration of previously made decisions. One project director engaged in developing and revising a logic model stated that

"... I am finding the creation of this model a never-ending process in the face of a deadline for submitting a proposal. Every time this model sits for a few days, someone sees something else that needs to be tweaked, and in the end we end up accomplishing little. And accomplishing nothing is our track record to date for evaluation, though there are folders marked 'logic model' and lots of paper trails."

Enhancing Communication Among Project Team Members

A second function of a logic model, closely related to the first, is enhancing communication among project team members. Obviously, engaging in a discussion of underlying program theory or what is really meant by an outcome area offers a new set of shared experiences for project team members, giving them a more solid basis for future discussion and decisions.

In addition, such discussion may also create enhanced ownership of the project, more buy-in to the ideas, and more accountability for seeing that it is carried out as intended. Team members working together to develop a shared definition of what success might look like can develop a greater investment in the outcomes. The disequilibrium that arises when a team member realizes that his or her vision of success is not the one shared by others can be replaced by a stronger bond and enhanced commitment if differences are resolved and a truly shared set of expectations is put in place.

For example, in one mathematics and science partnership program team members from the university and the partnering school systems were forced to discuss in some depth what the term *partnership* meant to them. Starting from such vague terms as "working together," "forming collaborations," or "participating in outreach," the discussion finally turned to considering factors such as:

- Whether there really were shared expectations for what the project would accomplish
- The benefits each expected to receive
- Anticipated roles and responsibilities with regard to decision making and implementation

- Events that reinforce trust, and events that create distrust
- Accountability—how, and to what extent, all partners accepted ownership for attainment of the varied goals

Discussing the partnership in these terms uncovered both areas of agreement and areas where the perceptions of the partners were far apart. Working through them helped to explain why some parts of the project seemed to falter and changed the communication patterns as the project moved forward.

Huebner (2000) suggests that in school settings logic model development can contribute to practice. Development of the model and discussion of the steps between the activities can encourage reflective practice—the process by which teachers actively think about their work and how it affects students. It also breaks down the isolation that is characteristic of teaching, affording an opportunity to share reflections and learn how others approach similar situations.

Having listed the multiple benefits that can arise with regard to communication and ownership, we feel it is also important to point out that the outcome of this communication may not always be positive. If differences are not resolved, if the team members hold their ground and cannot find a shared resolution, development of the logic model can rupture the ties that have bound the team together. Even if shared solutions are identified, the acrimony that might arise on the way to reaching that solution can leave a scar that is difficult to erase.

MANAGING THE PROJECT

A logic model can also lay the groundwork for project management. Once the theory of change is spelled out, managers can identify key points that need to be tracked to ensure that (1) activities are being carried out in a timely fashion and (2) problems are not allowed to continue unnoticed.

Working from the logic model, the manager can develop a schedule for activities and an anticipated schedule for when changes might be expected to occur. In essence, the logic model leads directly to development of a work plan with related deadlines and responsibilities. The logic model can also be a way of identifying contingencies between and among activities, acting as the starting point for developing powerful systems of project management. It is important to recognize, however, that a logic model is not in and of itself a management plan. The model can be used to scaffold a work plan or action plan, but it does not take the place of such a management tool.

Using a logic model in this way requires, however, that clear statements be made about when a next step or an activity is supposed to take place and when the results of that activity might reasonably be expected. The former is usually relatively easy to specify, but setting the schedule for expected results can be far trickier. It is not uncommon for an initial result of a treatment or change to be disequilibrium, an apparent step backward rather than forward. Specifying how long such disequilibrium should last and when hoped-for-results should be expected to occur can be a significant challenge.

Designing an Evaluation Plan and Determining the Questions to Be Addressed

A major reason for using logic models, and the main focus of this book, is the role they can play in laying the foundation for a comprehensive and meaningful evaluation. The Appendix presents an overview of the phases in developing an evaluation; it shows how a logic model fits into these phases. Before starting to develop an evaluation plan, it is extremely useful for the evaluator to develop a logic model for the project, if one has not already been created. Through the development, or examination, of a logic model, the evaluator can increase his or her understanding of what the project is trying to do and the strategies being used to address these ends. If the underlying logic of the project is not clear, it is always advisable to ask the questions needed for clarification before attempting to construct an evaluation approach.

Once the logic model is developed and understood, the parts of the model set out important guideposts for the evaluation and the questions that might be addressed. The activities or strategies identify opportunities for formative evaluation, assessing implementation and whether or not the plan is proceeding as envisioned. The outcomes identify results that must be examined in the summative evaluation. Expected time frames for the work give guidance to the evaluator as to when certain features of the project should be assessed.

Developing a logic model also serves as a means for forming relationships between the evaluator and the project. Huebner (2000) points out that if an evaluator works with the project team to develop a logic model, the understanding that develops between the evaluator and team members greatly benefits the ongoing work. If carried out appropriately, the development creates a nonthreatening situation in which all involved clarify the theory of change together. It also allows the participants the opportunity to point out what may be different or special in the particular context of the implementation—features of the project that may be well understood by the project team but not by the evaluator. It fosters an opportunity for the team to teach the evaluator and for the evaluator to raise questions before data are collected and there is any intimation that a judgment is being made.

Working with a team in this way requires a delicate balance between the role of the evaluator as a student and the role of the evaluator as a critical friend. If the evaluator appears to be too much of a student, project staff may come to question whether or not the evaluator has sufficient expertise to fulfill the expected evaluation role. If the evaluator raises too many questions about the project and its theory, project staff may become defensive and even begin to develop a sense of distrust. Further, if the evaluator's questions lead the project to make significant changes in plans, the role of the evaluator as an external, unbiased assessor may become compromised.

DOCUMENTING A PROJECT AND HOW IT WORKED

A logic model can also be used to document a theory of change after a project has been completed and its results obtained. Used in this way, the logic model becomes a map that guides others who may want to replicate the project or adapt it to other situations.

Sometimes this documentation may in actuality be updating an initial logic model, if the model was begun at an earlier point. Even if no previous model exists, developing one to capture the end product can be an important contribution to understanding what works and why.

Although an added step, it would be useful (and contribute to the knowledge base) to also document theories of change that did not quite work. Using a family of logic models to show theories of change that were attempted but failed can surface information that all too frequently is kept private. This documentation would be especially useful if reasons for the failure can also be offered and explanations offered for why the theory or theories did not hold.

EXAMINING A PROGRAM OR CONSTELLATION OF PROJECTS

Although our focus in this book is on the use of logic models for evaluation of individual projects, they can also be used to examine. By program we mean a group of projects being undertaken to fulfill a set of shared *program* goals. A logic model can be used to describe the theory of change underlying the program and address all the functions we have described for a project—clarifying what it is about, enhancing communication, managing the program, as well as scaffolding its evaluation.

Although in some cases the program logic model and a project's logic model may look alike, when a program contains various project types the logic model permits a look at the portfolio; one use of the logic model is to examine the portfolio in terms of balance, depth, and breadth.

For example, a program run by a federal agency has as its goal the advancement of knowledge about teaching and how to support high-quality teaching, along a continuum from motivating talented students to become teachers to continuing to support and use the expertise of master teachers. Underlying the program is a philosophy that posits success will require investment at each critical stage of the continuum and projects should be supported that address both research and demonstration. Development of a logic model can clarify assumptions regarding expectations for the portfolio, such as the relative emphasis on developing new teachers versus supporting those that are already in the field, targeting of the program to those serving early learners to those serving more mature learners, emphasis on service delivery rather than product development, and so on. The logic model can also help program managers map out which interactions, if any, are expected to occur among the types of investment and at what point in the program's evolution they should be become visible.

SUMMARY

Logic models have many uses and can serve the needs of various audiences. When done at the planning stage, such models help clarify what a project is about and identify problems before they become barriers to success. At the end of a project, a logic model can be a powerful tool for documenting what has been accomplished and why. Logic models are useful to a team that needs to understand and own a project, a manager who needs to monitor a project, and an evaluator who is asked to assess a project. Logic models can be applied to a single self-contained effort or used to describe a portfolio of projects intended to be complimentary in various ways. Used effectively and carefully, logic models afford greater clarity and understanding of sometimes ill- or incompletely defined interventions. Sometimes, however, the issues that logic models raise pose problems in and of themselves.

QUESTIONS TO CONSIDER

1. A variety of stakeholders can use logic models, not just evaluators. Considering the possible usages of logic models described in this chapter, discuss how funders, human resource specialists, and program managers might be able to use the tool. Which usages would be primary? Which ones secondary?
2. Think about projects you have been involved in or read about. Identify some examples of team members using the same words or terms but meaning different things. What kinds of problems did this cause? Why did this happen?

3. Discuss the pros and cons of the evaluator being involved in discussion with the project staff to help clarify what the team hopes to accomplish and what will be defined as success. Does this present any conflict of interest, or threaten the role of the evaluator as an external agent? Under what conditions would such discussion be considered appropriate and inappropriate?

CHAPTER THREE

THE COMPONENTS OF A LOGIC MODEL

This chapter presents details on exactly what is meant by a logic model and the key features that it contains.

- The major focus is on defining and discussing the four basic components of a logic model—inputs, activities, outputs, and outcomes—and noting critical distinctions.
- Optional additional components are also introduced.
- How models may differ in complexity is illustrated.

THE BASIC COMPONENTS OF A LOGIC MODEL

A logic model is a way of visually depicting the theory of change underlying a program, project, or policy. Figure 3.1 presents the basic components of a logic model.

A logic model consists of four basic components:

1. *Inputs.* The resources that are brought to a project. Typically, resources are defined in terms of funding sources or in-kind contributions.
2. *Activities.* The actions that are undertaken by the project to bring about desired ends. Some examples of activities are establishing community councils, providing professional development, or initiating a new information campaign.

FIGURE 3.1.   BASIC COMPONENTS OF A LOGIC MODEL.

| Inputs ⟶ Activities ⟶ Outputs ⟶ Outcomes |

3. *Outputs.* The immediate results of an action; they are services, events, and products that document implementation of an activity. Outputs are typically expressed numerically.
4. *Outcome.* Changes that occur showing movement toward achieving ultimate goals and objectives. Outcomes are desired accomplishments or changes.

Each of these components can be thought of as a part of the theory of change that was discussed in the previous chapter. Indeed, the parts of a logic model amount to the scaffolding for expressing the theory of change. The model shows what was done, to reach what ends, by whom, and with what resources.

Let's look more closely at each of these components and discuss some of the things that need to be considered in actually developing a logic model. Before doing so, however, it is important to stress that even though the exhibit suggests a conceptualization proceeding from left to right (inputs to outcomes), in building a logic model and describing a theory of change it is really more useful to start with specifying outcomes, not inputs. The thinking process works best by starting from what it is you want to accomplish and then moving to how you plan to get there. We start, therefore, with a discussion of outcomes.

Outcomes are the changes you want to see take place if your theory of change is accurate. They are the changes that document the success of a project. Examples of outcomes are changes in what students know and can do, or in a community's ability to solve significant problems, or in a medical practitioner's ability to reduce the prevalence of targeted diseases.

Outcomes can be situated at a variety of levels. In educational projects outcomes frequently focus on changes that happen to individuals or groups of individuals, but logic models may also be developed to address outcomes for institutions or communities. Take for example capacity building, a desired outcome in many projects. This outcome has meaning at the individual, community, and institutional levels. Projects that focus on individuals may have as an objective increasing individual capacity through provision of new skills and knowledge. Projects that focus on communities may have a capacity goal that addresses a group's ability to work together to solve a social problem. Projects that focus on institutions may have a capacity goal that is expressed in terms of changes in an infrastructure.

Outcomes also have an important time dimension. Most logic models distinguish among short-term, medium-term, and long-term outcomes. Though there is no hard-and-fast rule for how to quantify these durations, *short* frequently means two years or less; *medium*, more than two years and less than five years; and *long*, five years or greater. Part of establishing a theory of change is to articulate what changes you would expect to see in what time frame, if the underlying program theory is correct.

Activities describe the treatments or strategies that are undertaken to reach a desired outcome. Strategies are articulated steps, or the *what* of a program. Activities have several features. First, they are things that are done; they have a content. Second, in all but the simplest situations activities are not simultaneous but have an ordered sequence. Activities have a time dimension. In some projects, activities are also dependent and interdependent. What happens as a result of one activity may influence the shape of another activity. Third, activities are decomposable; as systems theory has said, there are systems within systems. What this means is that in developing a logic model there are many grain sizes that may be considered, from the global to the minute, depending on the lens brought to the system being examined.

One of the biggest challenges in constructing a logic model is deciding on the grain size for the activities being described. If it size is too large—say, for example, an activity is described as "professional development"—then too many events or products could be used as affirmation of successful implementation. If the grain size is too small—if each instance of professional development is described as a separate activity (identifying trainers, developing the curriculum for the initial session, developing the curriculum for the second session, training the trainers, scheduling the sessions, recruiting teachers, notifying teachers of the sessions, etc.) then the task of developing and testing a logic model could seem endless. Further, the resulting visual would in all likelihood be too cluttered to read or permit coherent guidance.

Outputs are the simplest and most immediate indicators of the progress of your theory. An output is a confirmation that one of the steps in the theory of change has been taken and that some product has resulted. Outputs are tied directly to activities, and each activity must have one or more outputs. Conversely, each output must be linked to one or more activities. Because outputs are essentially driven by activities, they also vary in grain size, with it being commensurate with the associated activity.

It is important to point out that distinguishing between outputs and outcomes can be a challenge; what is an output in one situation may be a legitimate outcome in another. We return to this topic later in our discussion.

Finally, inputs describe where the program starts in terms of the resources it has to work with. Though not exactly part of the theory of change, inputs describe the material and intellectual goods available to support the theory of change. Such resources include funds from a granting agency or agencies as well as other resources that are brought to support the project. Funds are almost always one of the critical inputs, but other nonmonetary supports are also frequently described. They may include the research base, previously established relationships among project partners, or accumulated craft knowledge that is special to the partners. Tangibles may also be counted as inputs. Typical tangibles are facilities, equipment, and other necessary tools.

Resources may seem somewhat outside the theory of change, but for a number of reasons it is important to be clear about the resources a project starts with. First, clarifying the availability of supports is important to all project partners, including the evaluator. Second, specifying the resources available is important for others who might want to replicate the project. If substantial resources are needed to support a given project, this should be communicated clearly to those wishing to undertake, and be successful in, similar endeavors in the future.

Let's take a simple project with a relatively straightforward theory of change and use it to illustrate development of a simple logic model.

The CDC wishes to increase awareness of the need for annual bone density tests for women over fifty-five. The ultimate goal of this project is to reduce the number of women who develop osteoporosis and suffer from broken bones through falls and other accidents. To do so, a campaign is initiated to share information about osteoporosis, its causes, and what a woman should do to protect herself from this disease. It is believed that a multifaceted approach will be effective, including a media campaign with television ads and radio announcements as well as written materials disseminated through libraries and grocery stores. If the theory holds true, it is expected that there will be an increase in calls or visits to doctors involving concerns related to osteoporosis. A secondary result should be an increase in awareness of osteoporosis and the problems that result. Ultimately, the percentage of women in this age range who have accidents related to osteoporosis should decrease.

The basic components of a logic model for this project is presented in Figure 3.2.

In this example, we have one input: funds provided by the CDC for the campaign. There are two activities: a media campaign and fact sheets. The outputs relate quite directly to the activities. For the media campaign, the most direct output is the number of stations adopting or using the campaign; for the fact sheets, a direct output is the number that actually distribute the

FIGURE 3.2. SIMPLE PROJECT WITH BASIC LOGIC MODEL COMPONENTS.

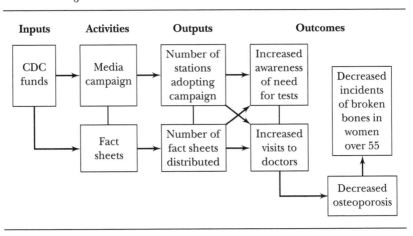

fact sheets. These examples of outputs help to illustrate the distinction between outputs and outcomes highlighted earlier. The outputs—stations using the media campaign and fact sheets being distributed—yield evidence that activities have been carried out; depending on how large these numbers are, they may suggest whether or not the approach is likely to be successful. However, *even a very large distribution of materials does not guarantee that the outcomes of the project will be achieved.* Distribution of information is not the same as the target audience understanding the information or making instrumental use of it. Outputs may in some sense offer evidence that planned activities have been accomplished, but examination of outputs is not sufficient and does not substitute for examining whether or not desired changes have occurred in an evaluation intended to say whether or not a treatment "worked."

The outcomes are multiple and occur at different points in time—changes in awareness and visits to the doctor occur; these changes are hypothesized to lead to an increase in visits to doctors or clinics and a general increase in public awareness regarding the need for such treatment. Lastly these short-term and medium-term outcomes are expected to lead to a decrease in osteoporosis and broken bones in the target group, women over fifty-five.

This example can also be used to illustrate how components are expressed in grain size. In the case illustrated here, the activities are presented at a high level of generality. A media campaign is not a single activity but the sum total of several subactivities that may include audience identification, theme development, theme test and revision, and product testing. An alternative display of components might use a more refined grain size showing both subactivities and suboutputs that are of interest (Figure 3.3).

Finally, although the example also appears to present the activities as being parallel, independent events, this is not necessarily the case. In reality, the fact sheets could be developed after the media campaign reached a certain level of maturity, and the more detailed logic model could show interdependence between the two sets of activities and the related time sequence. This issue of sequencing and how it is displayed is discussed more in the next chapter.

Figure 3.3. Simple Project with Detailed Breakdown of the Activity "Media Campaign and Related Outputs."

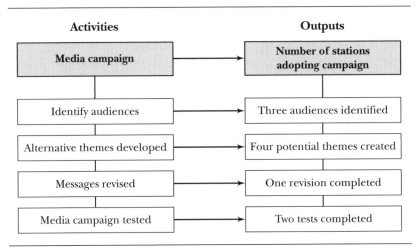

Additional Components in a Logic Model

So far this discussion has focused on the four components that go into logic models: inputs, activities, outputs, and outcomes. Two other components are frequently part of a logic model depiction. One is *context*; the other is called *impact*.

Context describes the important features of the environment in which the project or intervention takes place. It helps to define or delimit the circumstances to which the findings might be expected to generalize. Context frequently addresses the social, cultural, and political aspects of the environment. People factors such as race, gender, and socioeconomic status are one set of variables that might be considered under context. Community factors such as its racial, ethnic, religious, and economic makeup are also candidates. For many projects, political factors such as new educational mandates or change in high-level officials may also need to be considered.

Let's return to the CDC example that was discussed earlier and add some contextual features that might make a difference in how the project is developed and the situations to which the ultimate findings might be generalized. One contextual factor would be the primary language of the women to whom the campaign is directed. Let's assume that the community in which the project is being conducted is one in which the primary language is Spanish. Whether or not the strategy of a media campaign makes sense may depend on the availability of media outlets that issue information in the Spanish language. If the project is carried out in a community rich in such resources, the results might be quite different from those in a community where most media rely on English for expression. Another factor that might make a difference is the relative wealth or poverty of area in which the campaign is conducted. If the target population is relatively well to do, the plan of tracking visits to doctors may be appropriate. If, however, the targeted women come predominantly from lower-income families, seeking impact through visits to a doctor may not be the best strategy. If the campaign has an impact, it may be detected through visits to sources of wellness outreach other than doctors per se. There are many more contextual factors that could change the project in important ways, and ultimately change how the findings could be applied to other situations.

Context may not always relate to the demographics of a situation but instead reflect what might be considered the behavioral history of the situation. Subtler but equally important contextual factors may be found, for example, in previous experience with related projects. Where this history has been positive, the new project may be facilitated. If the related project left a residue of bad feelings or distrust, implementing a new project or intervention may face some special challenges.

Generally, the aspects of the context that need to be described are those factors that define the special features of the environment, features that might have to be considered in replication or generalization of findings.

According to the Kellogg Foundation (2000), impact is the intended or unintended change that occurs in a system, community, or organization that results from an intervention or a project. Related to the component outcomes, impacts are generally believed to be changes that affect a system more broadly and are sustained. If, for example, the goal of the CDC project described here was to revamp the health care system with regard to how osteoporosis is approached and treated, these changes would be treated as impacts in a logic model. Many education projects also focus on impacts, such as improving teacher quality through better preparation programs or more stringent entrance exams.

Even though attempting to address impacts is important, and many large-scale efforts have impacts as a goal, there are probably far more projects that do not aim quite this broadly. Many projects limit their goals to addressing a specific need at a specific point in time. Of the two additional components discussed here, evaluators are far more likely to need to address context than impacts. Figure 3.4 shows the logic model with context and impact added.

SUMMARY

A logic model consists of four basic components—inputs, activities, outputs, and outcomes—that describe a project's theory of change in terms of what is to be accomplished, using which strategies, and with what resources. The model can be developed

FIGURE 3.4. EXPANDED LOGIC MODEL.

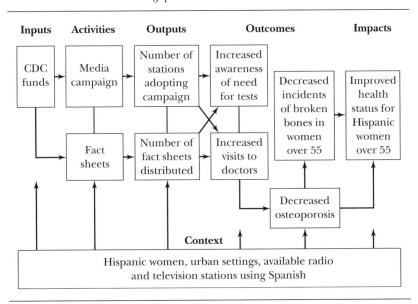

to varying degrees of detail, depending on the specific project and what is important to it. Logic models frequently also include descriptions of context—the specific conditions under which a project is carried out—and impacts—the effect of the project on a larger system.

In describing the components, it is important to understand the difference between outputs and outcomes and be clear about use of the information that comes from each.

QUESTIONS TO CONSIDER

1. Discuss the differences between outputs and outcomes. Can you think of a situation in which an output might also be an outcome?
2. Using several types of projects, such as a leadership program for principals or development of an alternative school, list what you think would be outputs and outcomes.
3. Taking the CDC example, identify (1) other inputs that might be important and (2) additional contextual features that might affect project implementation and the generalizability of findings.

CHAPTER FOUR

THE CONNECTIONS IN A LOGIC MODEL

In the previous chapter, the various components of a logic model were discussed. The chapter described the essential components of a logic model: inputs, activities, outputs, and outcomes. They relate the theory of change in terms of what is to be accomplished, using which strategies, and with what resources.

In this chapter, we complete our discussion of the layout of the logic model:

- We discuss what we call "connections" between and among components.
- We show the kinds of information that connections provide.
- We illustrate the importance of connections in adding the *why* and *how* to the logic model, filling out critical assumptions behind the particular theory of change.

CONNECTIONS AMONG COMPONENTS

A logic model consists of components and the connections among them. In the previous chapter, we focused on the components and described the content of each. However, it is the connections that really describe how things relate to one another and how the theory is expected to work. The simple logic model in Figure 4.1 (first presented in Chapter Three) used only limited, unidimensional connections to show how the major components of the model related to each other.

But connections are really far more complicated in most models, and it is accurate specification of connections that poses the greatest challenge.

We use the logic model presented in the previous chapter to illustrate connections (Figure 4.2).

There are two kinds of connection in this logic model: those showing the theory of change and those merely indicating that things are part of the same component. Where components are linked by a simple line, the connection shows that the items belong together as part of the same component. In our example, the media campaign and fact sheets are connected by a line to show that they are both part of the activity column; similar connections would be made between outputs of these activities (Figure 4.3).

The more critical connections are the ones showing how the components affect each other or interact to lead to the expected outcomes. These dynamic connections are typically portrayed

FIGURE 4.1. SIMPLE LOGIC MODEL.

Inputs ——————▶ Activities ——————▶ Outputs ——————▶ Outcomes

FIGURE 4.2. SIMPLE PROJECT WITH BASIC LOGIC MODEL COMPONENTS.

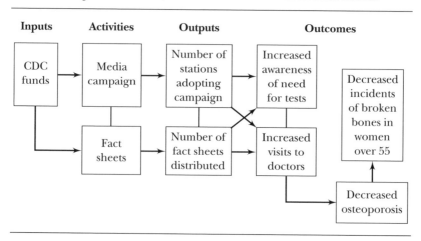

FIGURE 4.3. LOGIC MODEL SHOWING CONNECTIONS WITHIN COMPONENTS.

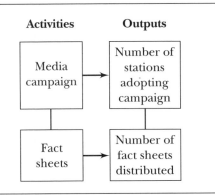

using an arrow revealing the direction of influence. It is important to realize that these directional connections are not just a kind of glue anchoring the otherwise floating boxes. Rather, they portray the changes that are expected to occur after a previous activity has taken place, and as a result of it. One part of the evaluation task is assessing whether the connections presented in the model can be confirmed. (This is discussed in more detail in Chapter Eight.) Here, we focus primarily on these dynamic connections that really detail the theory of change.

The first set of dynamic connections is shown in Figure 4.4; they are between inputs and activities. Here the connections describe the resources available to support the activities that are being undertaken by the project.

The connection between the inputs and the activities is fairly simple, with the inputs leading directly to both activities. Most projects operate on the notion that the resources available are not targeted differently according to the activity; they support the whole. Funds, for example, are used to support the whole range of activities that are carried out. If there were multiple inputs, with in-kind resources and community support also being part of the logic model, the principle would be the same (Figure 4.5). Although it is not impossible to think of an instance in which the connections between inputs and activities might be more fine-grained, the example portrayed here is typical.

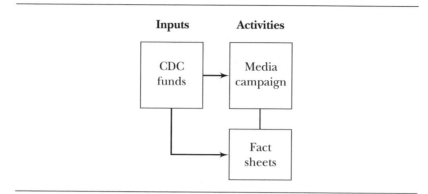

FIGURE 4.4. CONNECTIONS BETWEEN INPUTS AND ACTIVITIES.

FIGURE 4.5. CONNECTIONS BETWEEN MULTIPLE INPUTS AND ACTIVITIES.

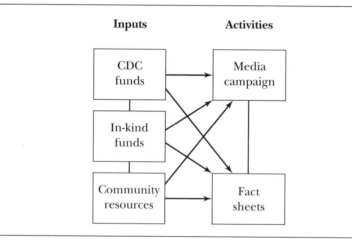

If all subcomponents in one component are linked to all subcomponents in another component, it is somewhat easier to show the relationship by simplifying the model as in Figure 4.6.

The two sets of brackets with the connecting arrow show that the theory of change posits all the inputs being expected to affect the activities in similar ways.

The second set of connections is between activities and outputs. These connections show what kind of product or accounting might furnish evidence that an activity has been implemented

FIGURE 4.6. SIMPLIFIED DISPLAY OF CONNECTIONS BETWEEN MULTIPLE INPUTS AND MULTIPLE ACTIVITIES.

FIGURE 4.6. SIMPLIFIED DISPLAY OF CONNECTIONS BETWEEN MULTIPLE INPUTS AND MULTIPLE ACTIVITIES.

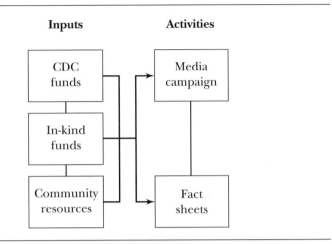

FIGURE 4.7. CONNECTIONS BETWEEN ACTIVITIES AND OUTPUTS.

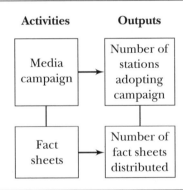

(Figure 4.7). For example, evidence that the media campaign has been implemented could be found in stations adopting and using the campaign. A somewhat different output is specified for the fact sheets; here the evidence is a simple count of the number of fact sheets distributed to various audiences.

The connections here show output or product that is expected to result from each activity. The output is directly tied to the specific activity such that the expected outputs of each activity can be differentiated. Remember, as stressed previously: these expected outputs say nothing about the quality or adequacy of the activity. They merely give evidence that something has happened. It is important to note that a logic model may show several outputs linked to a given activity. Conversely, more than one activity may link to the same output. Usually, however, it is preferable to have separate outputs for each activity. The correct portrayal depends on the particular theory of change you are trying to depict.

In our example, the simple logic model has one output for the activity "media campaign": the "number of stations adopting the campaign." A more complex model might include additional outputs such as the "number of times a day a spot is aired" or "the number of weeks the spot is presented." Including them as part of the project, the model would look like Figure 4.8.

In this model, dynamic connections are made between the activity of the media campaign and the three separate outputs.

Figure 4.9 illustrates a logic model with a flaw: not all necessary linkages have been illustrated. In this model, there is no output specified for the activity "fact sheets." Without having some way of acknowledging or documenting that this piece has been implemented, the theory of change is incomplete.

FIGURE 4.8. ACTIVITY WITH MULTIPLE OUTPUTS.

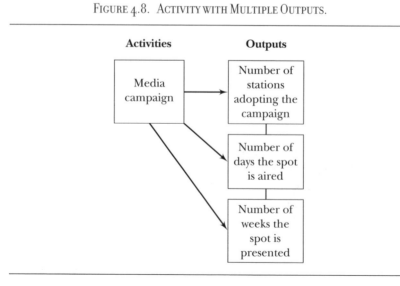

FIGURE 4.9. FLAWED LOGIC MODEL.

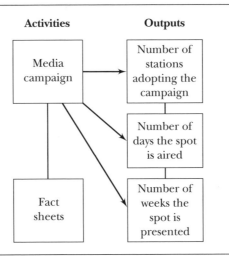

The third set of connections is between the outputs and outcomes, usually the short-term outcomes. This linkage connects the activity and its output to what is expected to be the earliest sign of change. Again, every output must link to one or more outcomes. Several outputs may link to the same outcome. For the simple case that we have been following, Figure 4.10 presents a logic model.

In this model, both activities and their outputs are intended to affect the same short-term outcomes. In this case, the activities

FIGURE 4.10. CONNECTIONS TO SHORT-TERM OUTCOMES.

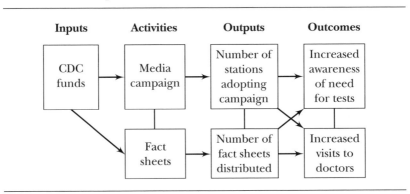

and outputs are linked to these outcomes similarly. However, it is important to realize that most projects are likely to have some activities expected to result in differing outcomes, at least in the short run. The logic model should show these short-term outcomes and relate them to particular activities, even if in the long run they are expected to contribute to the same outcome. A common error in developing logic models is to fail to differentiate among short-term linkages, instead simply linking all the activities to the cluster of outcomes, without making any distinctions among them. But if this is done, the theory becomes fuzzy and the full range of activities that need to be examined can be lost. Let's return to our example and see how this might play out.

Suppose that two other parts of the project are (1) an education campaign for community workers that makes them more familiar with the facts underlying the need for mammography and the signs of a possible problem, and (2) strategies for working with community members to help convince women to seek more frequent medical exams. The theory of change in this case suggests that both kinds of effort are necessary to achieve a long-term change in health prevention practices.

The logic model should now include separate short-term outcomes for the media campaign and fact sheets on the one hand and the education campaign on the other, to show what is expected from each and act as a guide for subsequent development of evaluation questions (Figure 4.11).

An incorrect depiction might take the form shown in Figure 4.12.

The two logic models have subcomponents, but in the first the connections between specific activities and outputs, and outputs and short-term outcomes, are portrayed more clearly and accurately and the theory of change is better represented. Unfortunately, a common error is to link each set of components in activities (or outputs) to each set of outcomes without appropriate specification.

It is also important to note that there may be some instances in which no short-term outcome can be identified. This is not typically the case, but the results of some activities may take longer to emerge than the results of others.

FIGURE 4.11. LOGIC MODEL ILLUSTRATING SHORT-TERM OUTCOMES.

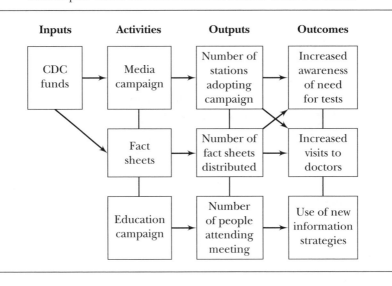

FIGURE 4.12. LOGIC MODEL WITHOUT CONNECTIONS APPROPRIATELY SPECIFIED.

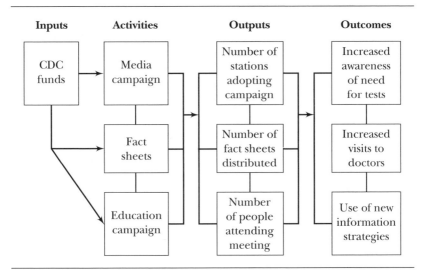

Finally, the logic model shows connections linking short-term outcomes to middle-term outcomes and middle-term outcomes to long-term outcomes (Figure 4.13).

Separating outcomes into time periods rather than aggregating them is not a matter of small consequence. In Figure 4.13, the theory states that both awareness and doctor visits should occur at about the same time and that there is no expectation that one precedes the other. Both are assumed to eventually lead to fewer broken bones in the long run.

Figure 4.14 sends a different message regarding the theory of change underlying the project, one affecting the design for the evaluation. Here the implication is that if the theory is true, awareness should occur first, then doctor visits, then decreased osteoporosis, and then fewer broken bones. The depiction also suggests a somewhat longer time frame for change to occur.

Feedback Loops

Earlier we talked about connections between subcomponents within a component. We showed a simple straight-line connection of these subcomponents and indicated that this line was not really dynamic but showed a kind of relationship within an activity. In some logic models, there are connections within or across components that illustrate another kind of expected interaction: a feedback loop. This is a connection showing how subcomponents may yield information that can confirm or disconfirm the adequacy of the project's operations. A feedback loop identifies where and when information gained from implementing one activity might be expected to affect what happens in another.

The importance of showing feedback loops depends on the project and what it is addressing. For multiyear or multiphase projects, where it is also expected that what is learned from initial implementation will lead to modification (or confirmation) of the treatment, planned feedback loops are very important. In the example of the CDC project, if the plan were to test out the media campaign and then revise it on the basis of the initial assessment of short-term outcomes, the model might look like Figure 4.15.

Here the feedback loop signals that information obtained through measurement of outputs—the number of stations airing

FIGURE 4.13. LOGIC MODEL WITH SPECIFICATION OF SHORT-TERM, MEDIUM-TERM, AND LONG-TERM OUTCOMES.

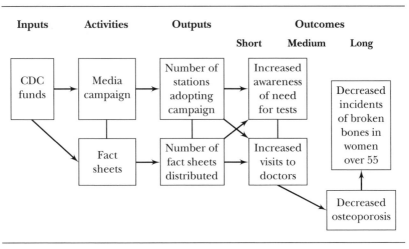

FIGURE 4.14. LOGIC MODEL WITH ALTERNATIVE SPECIFICATIONS OF SHORT-TERM, MEDIUM-TERM, AND LONG-TERM OUTCOMES.

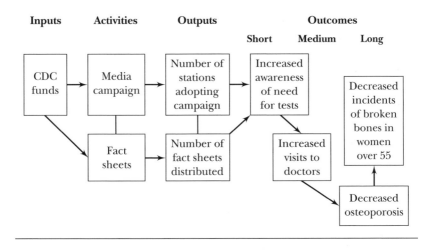

Figure 4.15. Logic Model with a Feedback Loop Among Activities, Inputs, and Short-Term Outcomes.

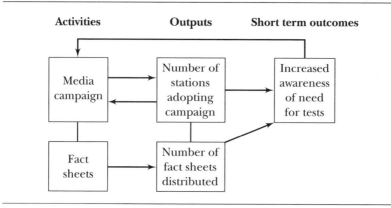

the campaign—and the short-term outcome "awareness" will be used to refine and modify the media campaign as necessary, if on initial implementation it is not sufficiently effective.

Summary

Connections play a critical role in articulating the theory of change in a logic model. They show how the various components relate and illustrate interactions and feedback that are expected to occur. A central part of a project is testing out whether or not hypothesized connections can be verified. Without verification of connections, the theory of change remains ambiguous; simply specifying components does not clarify the *why* or *how,* critical parts of both program description and program evaluation.

A constant challenge in developing logic models is to determine the level of detail for description or specification. With insufficient detail, the theory loses its explanatory power and the evaluation may well miss critical components. If too much detail is employed, the logic model can become overwhelming and the evaluation bogs down in minutiae. Most logic models benefit from having variation in detail, with some connections being more detailed than others. Prioritization of effort is essential.

Questions to Consider

1. Assume the CDC project includes these activities: a media campaign, fact sheets, and a home visitor component. The home visitor component is intended to be a third form of delivery mechanism to reach the same goals. It is critical in this activity to select appropriate personnel and offer training for them to make sure they have accurate understanding of the issues involved. Illustrate use of connections of differing grain sizes for the activities in a logic model. Explain why you have used larger and smaller grains.

2. For the same project, show a correct way and an incorrect way of making connections among multiple activities and their outputs.

3. Now add a feedback loop. How would you expect it to affect the project?

CHAPTER FIVE

DEVELOPING LOGIC MODELS TO SUPPORT EVALUATION

In this chapter, we discuss development of a logic model and some of the factors that come into play. We point out the interaction between logic model development and project development. A major theme of the chapter is that a logic model is a living tool. It can also be used as a screen in sorting through and trying to eliminate activities that may or may not be integral to the theory of change.

The discussion of logic model development is organized around these themes:

- *Teaming.* Drawing on understandings or program staff to create a logic model
- *Collaborative learning.* Developing a true shared understanding of the project and criteria for success through joint problem solving
- *Timing.* Revisiting and refining the logic model as experience brings new information

TEAMING

Logic model development is facilitated and enhanced if the process of development involves a team that includes, at a minimum, the project developers and the evaluators. Project developers and evaluators have their own skill sets, knowledge, and frequently different ways of thinking about the same set of activities, goals, and objectives. Simply put, developers tend to focus on the question of how best to do something; evaluators focus on the question of how best to assess whether the project is working as planned and the desired outcomes have been obtained. Working together, they can greatly enhance the product that results.

This emphasis on teaming does not mean that evaluators or project developers cannot develop a logic model independently, although this is far less likely to occur. Many times evaluators do take the first stab at logic model development, creating from their understanding of the project a depiction of components and connections that appear to describe the project's theory of change. But unless the logic model is validated against the understanding of those who are doing the work and have developed the idea, its accuracy and utility are likely to be diminished.

At the outset, it is important to develop a joint understanding of what is meant by a logic model. Just as Chapters Three and Four carefully explained the components and connections that make up a logic model, a similar overview and sharing of definitions should occur prior to logic model development. It is critical that everyone understand the difference between an output and an outcome. It is also important to understand the need for carefully articulated connections, if the model is going to illustrate the theory of change.

How can working together happen? There are a number of ways for teams to develop logic models. One is to have each person or a small number of people work together to develop their individual models and then compare the models that emerge. This is a good approach when all present really do have a good understanding of what a logic model is. If this is not the case, too much time may be spent on dealing with confusion in form and format, rather than creating a shared theory of change and debating difference in understanding. Teaching and applying the technique both present challenges; it is best not to try to accomplish the two ends at the same time.

A more productive way to work together is to specify the components and connections, correcting any misunderstandings in form and format if they are really a distraction. Starting from goal specification is a good idea; unless there is agreement on the goals, reaching agreement on activities will serve little purpose. Unfortunately, this is precisely the problem with a number of projects. Developers are much more articulate about what they want to do than about what they hope to achieve.

In addressing goals, it is helpful to try to reach agreement on a relatively macro level before moving to more explicit definition of exactly what and how. For example, if "student learning" is a desired outcome, during initial logic model development it is probably sufficient to qualify that the target is academic learning or enhancement of knowledge in mathematics and not spend too much time deciding whether the learning is documented through a course grade, a product, or a test score. Reaching consensus on which indicators of learning will be used is important, but this need not be accomplished at the beginning. Similarly, if a critical activity is "professional development for teachers," deciding who will deliver the professional development and what experiences will count as professional development can also be postponed.

The discussion that is bound to take place as components are defined and connections are articulated will be invaluable for both project implementation and evaluation design and refinement. It is common to have issues that arise in developing the logic model point to problems in the design of the project itself. The very act of developing a logic model can have an immediate impact on the project. Even the rabbit tracks that may appear to lead the discussion off course will have a pay-off in the long run. An example can help to illustrate this.

Evaluators and program developer were working together to develop a logic model for a teacher quality grant. As the discussion turned to one set of outcomes—establishing a 2 + 2 program (a program in which the last two years of high school are combined with two years of undergraduate education) at the partnering institutions—the discussion got bogged down as representatives from the institutions argued over their perceptions of whether or not policies at their institutions of higher education allowed transfer of credits from the initial two years of the program to the post-secondary level. After considerable energy was expended on how to handle the 2 + 2 situation in light of the apparent difference in policies under which they were operating, the team realized that they needed an added activity—policy review and development—and an added outcome—consistency in policy regarding acceptance of credits. Without this policy change, their efforts at developing the program and training teachers to implement it would be futile. Figures 5.1 and 5.2 show the first and second logic models that emerged from this discussion.

FIGURE 5.1. INITIAL LOGIC MODEL FOR TEACHER QUALITY GRANT.

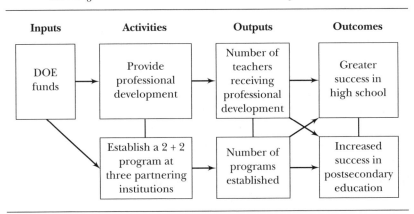

FIGURE 5.2. REVISED LOGIC MODEL FOR TEACHER QUALITY GRANT.

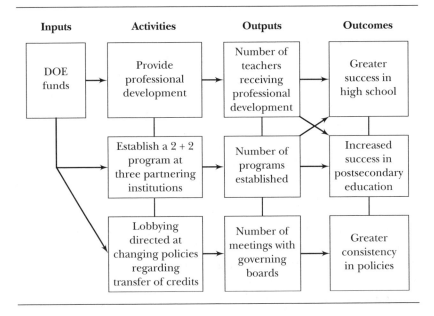

Collaborative Learning

The consensus that should result from developing a logic model addresses not only the theory of change but also how the presence or absence of that change will be recognized, and ultimately measured. The earlier discussion about laying out the basic components of a logic model urged participants not to rush into spelling out details too soon. It is important to get the overall structure in place before turning to the details that further define the structure. Postponing the discussion does not mean ignoring the discussion. The consensus process requires returning to the more detailed level of definition before the logic model can be considered complete.

What are the next steps? After the overall model is developed, it is important to return to the major constructs that are represented by the components and explore what the team members believe these constructs mean in concrete terms. Once agreement on definition is reached, the final step is to determine more precisely how measurement will occur. The process being undertaken is sometimes referred to as "operationalization," moving from a global definition of a concept or construct to specifying observables that should be examined.

In our example, we indicated that deferring a discussion of what is meant by student learning is probably strategic at the beginning of logic model development. Once the overall model is established, it is then time to return to a closer look at the outcome "student learning" and what it means to the team members. Is student learning the same thing as performance on a standardized test? a high-stakes test? another kind of assessment instrument? To what extent do the team members feel it is important to have multiple definitions (and multiple measures) for the outcomes? Should student learning be examined in terms of grades, products, and participation in challenging courses, as well as performance on tests?

Reaching agreement on a definition of student learning might be challenging, but the challenge is far less severe than when other, vaguer constructs must be operationalized. In an earlier example, the outcome of "changes in infrastructure" was found to emerge as a result of the logic modeling exercise. How can this construct be operationalized? One definition might be enhanced consistency of policies across institutions. If policies change and are enforced, the probability increases that any impact will spread beyond the groups immediately involved and be sustained over time. A second definition could address change in the capacity of individuals to carry out the work at hand. A third definition might be new models for delivering services that change what has been business as usual.

As the partners work together collaboratively to define what is meant by the terms in the logic model, new understandings will arise regarding exactly what is meant by the terms that have been included. These understandings will help the evaluators determine what needs to be measured, and ultimately, how to best measure the indicators of greatest interest.

Another example illustrates the role of collaborative learning in operationalizing terms so that they can be more accurately measured. Local Systemic Initiatives were started by the National Science Foundation as a way to enhance the quality of teaching in mathematics and science. Starting with elementary grade mathematics and science, the program eventually spread across the grade levels. Central to the theory of change underlying the program is the belief that extended, high-quality professional development, using a standards-based curriculum, will lead to enhanced teaching and improved student learning.

The original logic model for this project captures these key points; it is shown in Figure 5.3.

As this model was developed, a critical factor needing clarification was what would count as professional development.

FIGURE 5.3. LOGIC MODEL FOR LOCAL SYSTEMIC INITIATIVES.

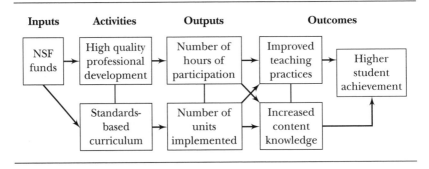

The program had a requirement that teachers receive at least 120 hours of professional development. The question then arose as to what kind of experience can be counted toward the 120 hour total. Debate centered around the role of some curriculum-related activities in which teachers might participate, such as development of curriculum guides or review of curriculum in light of state or district standards, participating in coaching or mentoring, and being part of a lesson study group. After somewhat heated discussion, a decision was finally reached as to what would be included and what would not. Before this decision was reached, it was not possible for the evaluator to complete the task of identifying measures and measurement procedures.

Timing

Earlier we discussed the fact that logic model development can occur at a variety of points in the evolution of a project: in the beginning, during, or at the end. Ideally a logic model should be developed as part of project design and planning, but it still has considerable utility if introduced after the project is under way. Developing a logic model to document what has been found at the end of a project can also make a contribution to the field.

Whenever the model is initially developed, getting it right, or close to right, will take time. The logic model probably has to be revisited and revised several times before there is agreement that the right components and connections have been called out. This can be a grueling and even frustrating task, but one that almost always reaps substantial rewards in the end. It is important to realize that this is a typical part of the process of documenting a project's underlying theory of change, a kind of deconstruction that ultimately results in construction of a more solid unit.

It is also important to realize that the model is not set in concrete but is subject to change over time; even a model developed at the end of a project may be modified by subsequent experience. The feedback loops discussed in the previous chapter are one specific source of impetus for change. Frequently, trying to implement a project causes activities to surface that may have been overlooked at the outset. Information coming from research on similar programs may also introduce new elements into the picture. If both time and resources are sufficient, it may be possible not only to refine the logic model but also to move forward with testing out the new model in a real-world situation. Evaluators and project developers need to recognize the importance of revisiting—and even challenging—an established model as the project unfolds.

SUMMARY

This chapter discusses some things to consider in developing a logic model and the benefits that can accrue. Several characteristics of logic model development are emphasized, notably that it is a team experience, it typically results in new understandings for those who participate, and it is an iterative and ongoing process. Benefits from applying the logic model framework can be found early on and may continue to appear as new information is incorporated.

QUESTIONS TO CONSIDER

1. Consider the example of the teacher quality project. Suppose the evaluator developed the logic model on her own and then simply gave it to the project team for verification. Do you think the team would realize that a piece was missing? Why or why not?
2. In this chapter, we have used the term *operationalize* several times. Discuss what it means to operationalize a construct. How would you operationalize outcomes such as "improved climate" or "a stronger partnership"?
3. The chapter stresses that a logic model is a living thing, that it changes over time. Why is this a strength? How might it also prove to be a weakness?

CHAPTER SIX

DEVELOPING LOGIC MODELS OF DIFFERING COMPLEXITY

In this chapter, we look more closely at the development of logic models for a variety of projects. We illustrate the utility of the tool for projects of differing complexity and how alternative theories of change might be constructed.

The examples have been constructed to offer a realistic picture of what evaluators might expect to encounter in working with stakeholder groups to develop a logic model. In later chapters, we follow up with a project discussed here and show how the logic model helps guide the evaluation questions that are developed.

PROJECT ONE

Blowdon Tech is developing a new basic course in systems theory that includes a unit on nanotechnology. The purpose of the course is to give undergraduates an introduction to nanotechnology and hopefully pique their interest in taking additional courses in this field. The project requires faculty in the engineering, biology, and business schools to work cooperatively in developing and implementing the course. It is hoped that this interaction will encourage faculty to work together on other courses or research projects.

The project is being partially supported by grants from the Flicker Foundation (a local charity) and the Business Roundtable. These groups hope that the work will result not only in improved academic preparation of students but also in more integration of cutting-edge knowledge into courses in general. In the long run, they see a successful project contributing to the quality of the workforce that will be available to the local community.

As a condition of the grant, the Flicker Foundation has required that the project have an external evaluation. Further, it has stipulated that an initial step in this evaluation should be development of a logic model that represents the joint understanding of the stakeholders.

The evaluator meets with the faculty to start developing a logic model for the project. They begin with the expected outcomes (Figure 6.1). Here is the faculty list:

- Development of a new course
- Increased enrollment in the basic systems course
- Increased enrollment in nanotechnology courses

The evaluator looks at these three outcomes and immediately notices two problems. First, one of the outcomes is really an output, rather than an outcome. That is, development of a new course, although an important part of the project, is not really the goal of the project. The goal is to influence the course-taking patterns of students. If all that is accomplished is creation of a new course, the faculty might consider this to be success but the funders will not have the same opinion. This is not an easy concept to grasp, and considerable discussion occurs as to why development of a new

FIGURE 6.1. INITIAL OUTCOMES.

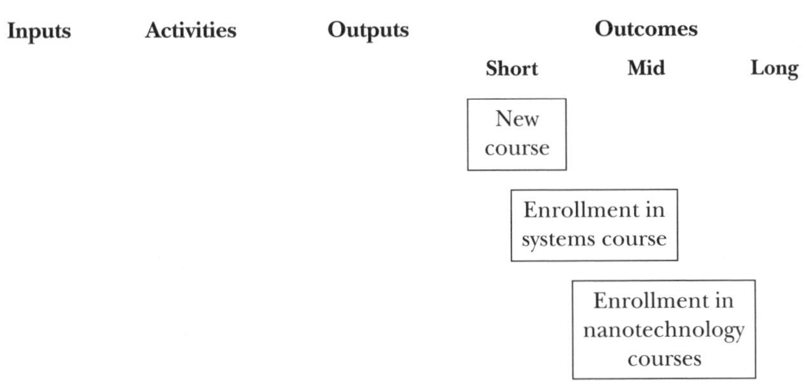

Inputs	Activities	Outputs	Outcomes		
			Short	Mid	Long
		New course			
			Enrollment in systems course		
				Enrollment in nanotechnology courses	

course is not considered a short-term outcome. Reluctantly the faculty accepts the notion that developing a course is an activity and creation of the course is an output.

The second problem is that the outcomes, as stated, say nothing about whether students become more interested in studying nanotechnology (an explicit goal of the project) or whether they became more knowledgeable (a goal of the funders who are hoping for a better prepared workforce). The faculty argue that enrollment in additional nanotechnology courses is the same as increased interest; the evaluator says it may be one indicator, but enrollment could occur for other reasons: perhaps because of scheduling issues, or because they were already interested in the field and the basic systems course had no effect. Considerable debate also ensues over whether or not student learning should be identified as a project outcome. The faculty is of two minds. Some feel learning doesn't need to be measured. To them, the important outcome is that the new information is being delivered. Others say that it is important and will be readily measurable by performance on the final exam. The expanded logic (Figure 6.2)

Figure 6.2.   Project Logic Model with Expanded Outcomes.

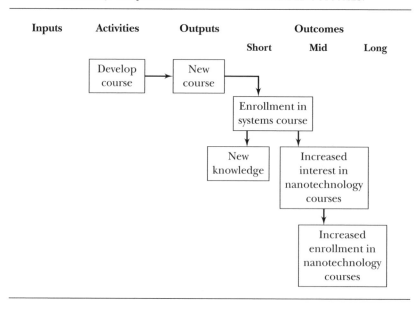

adds both interest and gaining new information as outcomes. It is agreed that this is a tentative decision and must be revisited.

It looks as though all that needs to be done is add the inputs—funds from the Flicker Foundation and the business community—and the logic model will be completed. However, a funder who happens to join the group at this point raises some questions. The logic model says nothing about who should be engaged in developing the course. As is, the theory of change does not acknowledge that course development requires the collaboration of three groups who typically do not interact: faculty from the engineering, biology, and business schools. She suggests that some note be made of this expectation in the model and that potential long-term effects on collaboration also be added to the model. The faculty are somewhat uncomfortable with this suggestion, but they are persuaded that it should be added because it seems so important to a key stakeholder. The resultant model is seen in Figure 6.3.

FIGURE 6.3. PROJECT LOGIC MODEL WITH LONG-TERM IMPACT.

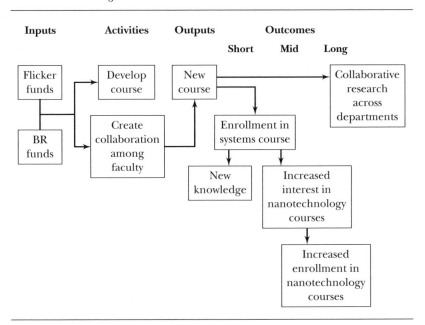

At this point, one of the faculty suggests that a long-term goal might be to get more funding to develop new courses. This is said only partially in jest, but other faculty seem to agree that it should be added. The evaluator suggests that even though faculty may hope that additional funding ensues it is not a goal of the project to secure additional funds for the faculty, and this outcome is inappropriate.

Project Two

The Chelsea Public Schools are initiating a new program to assist middle school students in acquiring literacy skills. Aimed especially at students who are reading two or more years below grade level, the program combines professional development, coaching by mentor teachers, and a supplemental reading program to enhance the skills of the targeted students. Staff members feel that these three components are necessary if project goals are to be met and that they need to be seen as mutually supportive and integrated. A special feature of this program is involvement of university faculty in developing and delivering the professional development. It is expected that disciplinary faculty will bring to the project a depth of content knowledge that is all too often missing in professional development sessions.

Working with university faculty and the district's staff development team, the coordinator of reading has laid out a three-year cycle designed to (1) increase teachers' understanding of what research has to say about effective literacy instruction for middle school students and (2) enhance their skills. This partnership between the university and the school district is seen as critical in ensuring that teachers are exposed to rich, accurate content, as well as appropriate pedagogy. The district is also able to use Title I funds to support the program.

Starting with three of the district's nine middle schools, the program will be examined over a three-year period. All teachers will be included, because it is believed that the program will be of benefit to veteran teachers as well as new ones. Extension of the program to other schools will be determined on the basis of available resources and the results of the initial three-year study. It is expected that by the end of the first three years significant increases will be seen in students' reading achievement, interest in reading, and confidence in self as a reader.

The Chelsea Public Schools are located in the southwestern United States. This is a medium-sized school district, serving approximately thirty thousand students. The school population is 50 percent Caucasian, 35 percent Hispanic, 10 percent African American, and 5 percent Asian. The population is considered working-class, with an average of 45 percent of students receiving free or reduced-price lunch in the nine middle schools.

The local university is a four-year college that generally serves students from the surrounding area. The departments have not ordinarily given direct assistance to local school districts, although preservice education is an important part of the university program. New policies at the college aimed at encouraging outreach were the impetus for the cognitive studies department to become involved with the Chelsea district. However, recruiting university faculty and creating a partnership between the faculty and the K–12 staff is acknowledged to be a new challenge. Both sides know that for the project to be successful it will be essential to establish a mutually beneficial partnership.

The evaluator, the coordinator of reading, Chelsea staff development team members, and university faculty gather to develop a logic model for the program. Because few staff members have used logic models before, the evaluator develops an initial logic model that will be a starting point. This logic model (Figure 6.4) shows what is expected over the three-year time frame of the project.

Starting with what the project is expected to accomplish, the evaluator identifies outcomes:

- Three long-term outcomes relating to students: higher achievement in reading, increased confidence in self as a reader, and increased interest in reading
- An intermediate outcome: increased use of inquiry teaching practices (a teacher outcome)
- A short-term outcome: changes in teacher content and pedagogical knowledge

The arrows in the figure show that these outcomes are expected to occur in a sequence:

FIGURE 6.4. READING PROJECT LOGIC MODEL.

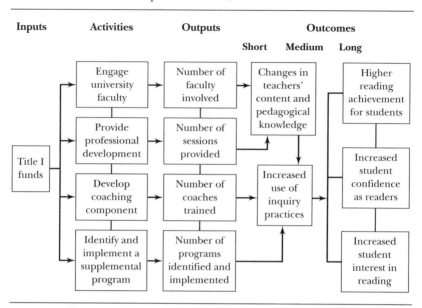

1. Teachers will show a change in knowledge.
2. This change will lead to increased use of inquiry practices in teaching
3. At the end of the three years, these changes in teaching are expected to lead to the three student outcomes of achievement, confidence, and interest.

Four activities are identified in the model:

1. Engaging university faculty
2. Providing professional development
3. Coaching
4. Identifying and implementing a supplemental program of instruction

As the arrows show, faculty engagement and professional development are both expected to result in changes in teacher knowledge. These activities, combined with coaching and the new program, are also expected to have a direct impact on the use of inquiry teaching practices.

Finally, the evaluator identifies Title I resources as a critical input and draws an arrow to show how this resource affects all of the activities in the model.

The group meets to review the model. The first question that arises relates to outcomes. The lead staff developer thinks that some outcomes are missing; specifically, she wants to add development of a new model for staff development that involves both K–12 and university faculty. She sees this systemic impact as an important goal of the project. The team debates whether or not to add the model development as a program impact. Ultimately, they decide that even though developing such a model would be desirable they don't feel it is feasible to do so within the three-year time span of the project. This modification is not made.

The coordinator of reading looks at the student outcomes and raises the question of whether or not they are all long-term outcomes and would be expected to occur at the same time. She suggests that their theory of change assumes a temporal sequence that isn't captured by the current depiction. According to her reasoning, the outcome portion of the logic model would be more accurate if it showed increased inquiry leading to increased confidence, confidence leading to increased interest in reading, and these two outcomes leading to higher achievement (Figure 6.5).

The evaluator explains that this is an important modification and affects which types of change are looked for and at what time period. Further, the assumption that increased confidence and interest come before, and lead to, changes in achievement becomes an important part of the theory to be empirically examined. Others working on the logic model are initially supportive of this revision, but debate soon arises with regard to exactly what order would be expected, and whether indeed higher achievement is the end result of the other changes or a precursor instead. Much time is spent on this issue and the implications of one path or another for the project. The coordinator of reading holds fast to her belief in the sequence. Others are just as steadfast in their belief that alternative expectations for the sequencing of outcomes should be held. The resolution is to return to the original depiction in which the outcomes are assumed to occur at about the same time and see what can be learned from the project regarding which sequence(s) to expect.

FIGURE 6.5. READING PROJECT LOGIC MODEL WITH SEQUENCED STUDENT OUTCOMES.

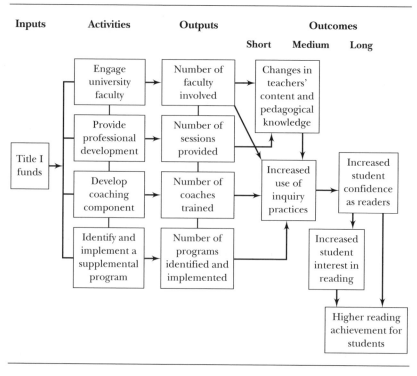

The logic model leads to other discussion when activities and their associated outputs are considered. A major question is whether or not involvement of faculty is supposed to lead to changes in both teacher knowledge and use of inquiry practices. Faculty will be involved in developing the curriculum for the professional development and delivering some of the sessions. However, from the faculty's point of view, their involvement will primarily address content knowledge; they do not see themselves making a major contribution to changes toward inquiry-based practices. Indeed, if the expectation is that faculty will address this area, some further discussion is required because this is not their understanding. Some in the group take exception to this delimitation of the faculty's role; most agree that increased use of inquiry practices is most directly affected by the coaching component and the new supplemental program, as well as the pedagogical portion of the professional development. They finally agree that the arrow connecting faculty engagement to increases in inquiry-based teaching practices should be removed for now (Figure 6.6), but that this issue will need revisiting as the project is developed.

The discussion of activities—especially of faculty engagement—also raises some issues with regard to the potential interaction among the activities. As depicted here, it appears that the activities work in parallel and do not affect each other. There is strong objection to this notion, and representatives from both the school system and the university stress the importance of interactions among the activities themselves. Key among them is the role that faculty are supposed to play in professional development,

Figure 6.6. Project Logic Model with Clarification of Expectations for Faculty Involvement.

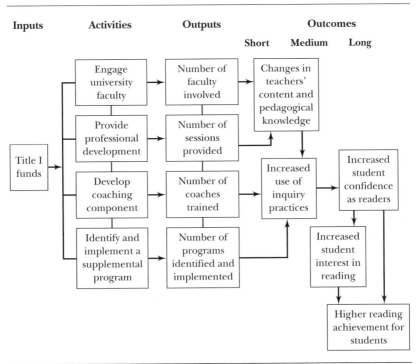

both in design and delivery. Without the involvement of faculty in designing and delivering the professional development sessions, the project will be quite different. Similarly, there is an expected interaction between professional development and the supplemental program. The former is expected as the major vehicle for helping the teachers learn to implement the latter. Another set of modifications to the model is then proposed (Figure 6.7), showing the importance of the interactions among the parts.

Finally, the group addresses the inputs. Little disagreement is raised with regard to the role of Title I funds, but some suggest that valuable inputs from the school system and the university need more explicit recognition. They state that without expertise from these two organizations, the project cannot be undertaken. The decision is made to add them to the logic model.

FIGURE 6.7. PROJECT LOGIC MODEL WITH INTERACTIONS SHOWN.

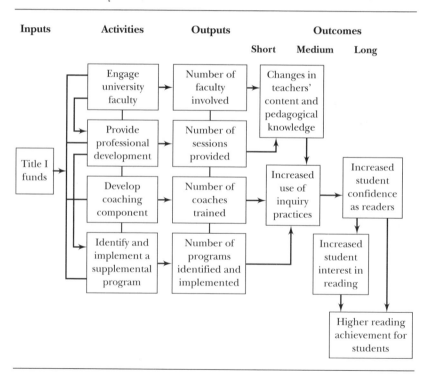

It looks as if the task of developing the logic model is completed when Chelsea school staff raise some additional questions. How about selecting and recruiting three schools to be part of the new approach? Although it would be possible to simply mandate that three schools try the new approach, staff argue that it would be better to try to get schools to agree to be part of the project. If schools feel they have a choice and can elect to be in the project because they feel the new approach is beneficial to them, the chances of the project's success are enhanced. It appears to save time to mandate participation, but in the long run this might not prove to be effective. Given this discussion, although the original plan did not address how schools would be selected, the decision is to try to recruit schools and get their buy-in rather than requiring schools to participate. The logic model is revised again, with the result shown in Figure 6.8.

FIGURE 6.8. COMPLETED GENERAL PROJECT LOGIC MODEL.

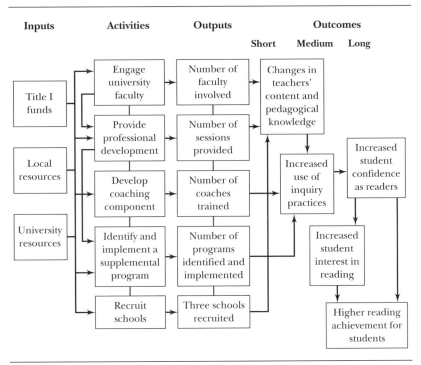

SUMMARY

These examples of logic model development help to highlight the challenges and benefits of the process:

- Project staff frequently confuse outputs with outcomes. It may take some time to help them understand the difference (for example, developing a new course).
- All stakeholder perspectives need to be considered in developing a logic model. However, the expectations of certain stakeholders (funders) may be more important than those of others.
- It is important to distinguish between project goals and personal goals (gaining additional funding).
- Developing a logic model helps to reveal perceptions that might otherwise surface at an inopportune time (such as expectations regarding the contribution of faculty to changing teacher practices).
- Carefully examining the connections among outcomes clarifies differences in the theories of change held by particular partners (as in whether or not to sequence the student outcomes).
- Developing a logic model may uncover components of the project that must be addressed differently (whether to mandate or recruit schools for participation).
- Logic model development takes time and careful attention to all the pieces.

QUESTIONS TO CONSIDER

1. Consider the theories of change portrayed with regard to Project Two. Which one do you find most compelling, and why?
2. Assume that a goal of Project One was to increase the diversity of students enrolled in nanotechnology courses. What impact would this have on the activities and goals of the logic model?

CHAPTER SEVEN

USING A LOGIC MODEL TO IDENTIFY EVALUATION QUESTIONS

For the evaluator, the purpose of building a logic model is primarily to lay the foundation for developing or refining an evaluation plan. Although it is clear that such a model can make a major contribution to designing and implementing a project, it is the role that a logic model can play in evaluation that makes the model so important for the evaluator. In this chapter, we first discuss how a logic model can be used in evaluation, and then we look more closely at how it can be used in guiding development of evaluation questions.

THE RELATIONSHIP BETWEEN LOGIC MODELING AND EVALUATION

Earlier we described a logic model as a tool to scaffold an evaluation plan. A logic model is not an evaluation approach, or an evaluation design, or an evaluation system. It is a tool that helps to clarify the critical components and linkages within a project, offering a blueprint of possible areas on which an evaluation might focus.

Let's take an educational intervention project that we discussed earlier and see how the logic model helps the evaluator develop an appropriate evaluation approach.

The Chelsea Public Schools district is initiating a new literacy program for middle school students who read two or more years below grade level. The program has three components: professional development, coaching, and supplemental reading intervention to enhance the skills of the targeted students. A special component of the program is the joint participation of university faculty and school district staff. This partnership between the university and the school district is seen as critical in assuring that teachers are exposed to rich, accurate content, as well as appropriate pedagogy. The pilot program will be implemented in three schools over a three-year period.

Working together, the evaluator and the project team have developed an overall logic model. It is somewhat complex because each major class of activity must be broken down into critical component parts. For example, professional development includes not just subcomponents related generally to design, development, and implementation but also subcomponents that address the roles of the partners in the professional development system. That is, in this project there are some specific reasons for including both university faculty and school-based experts. Faculty are expected to provide expertise in the content, while school staff take the lead in pedagogy. In addition, the faculty are expected to be engaged in development of the lessons as well as expected to work directly with the teachers. This involves presentation of materials, classroom observations, and mentoring. Figure 7.1 is the logic model for this project that was developed earlier.

Once the model is developed, the evaluator is ready to turn to the evaluation design. Given the nature of the project, it is important that both formative and summative studies be undertaken. Thus the evaluator will develop a plan that examines whether or not the program is being implemented as designed, whether there is evidence of progress toward identified outcomes (formative evaluation), and whether the goals of the project are reached at the end of the three-year period (summative evaluation).

IMPLEMENTATION

The logic model (specifically, the components listed under the activities) is a starting point for identifying questions to ask about program implementation. Five potential areas for formative evaluation can be identified:

Figure 7.1. General Project Logic Model.

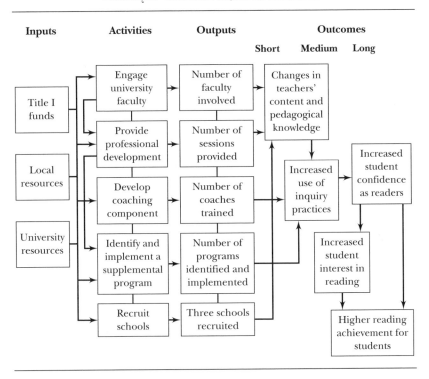

1. Have schools been recruited and teachers identified for participation?
2. Are the faculty engaged and supported?
3. Has the professional development program been implemented and coaching put in place?
4. Has the supplemental intervention been carried out?

An important part of this logic model is the importance placed on faculty involvement. Discussion between the evaluator and the project staff undertaken as the logic model was being built pointed out that the role of faculty was believed to be a key component of the program; full and genuine engagement of disciplinary experts was seen as essential.

Once the blueprint is completed, the evaluator needs to examine the possible opportunities for evaluation and determine on which ones effort will focus. It is seldom possible to evaluate each and every component and linkage that the logic model depicts. However, it is important in the early stages of evaluation development to think comprehensively and broadly. Narrowing down and prioritizing questions is a subsequent step.

A first step is usually to sketch out the areas that the evaluation might examine. The formative implementation areas can be taken directly from the "activities" column of the logic model (Figure 7.2). They are recruitment, partnership formation, delivery of professional development, coaching, and implementation of a supplemental curriculum.

FIGURE 7.2.   USING ACTIVITIES TO DEFINE A STARTING POINT
FOR FORMATIVE EVALUATION.

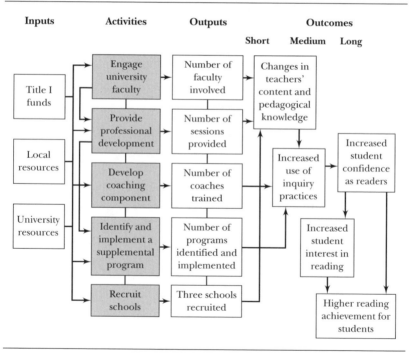

Each activity can be represented in the evaluation design by simple questions, such as:

- Was the recruiting carried out as planned?
- Were faculty engaged as planned?
- Was professional development delivered as planned?

However, phrasing evaluation questions in this way is probably not adequate; questions posed at this level of generality do little to draw on the information contained in the logic model and address the underlying theory of change only superficially. Starting with these broad questions as a kind of outline, and using the understanding of the project that evolved during logic model development, the evaluator typically breaks down each question into specific subquestions that more clearly define what it is that needs to be examined.

Taking professional development as an example, we pose some likely questions:

- Did designing professional development units involve both university faculty and school-based staff?
- Was appropriate attention paid to the needs of special student groups such as English language learners? Were key content areas that research has identified as important covered adequately?
- Was the design completed in a timely manner?
- Was attention paid to explicating and establishing the roles of university faculty and schools staff in delivering the units?
- Was professional development provided as designed with regard to schedule, coverage of material, and roles played by university faculty and school-based staff? Did the professional development sessions build on what is known about best practices in teaching adult learners? Did the professional development sessions afford an appropriate balance of theory and practical applications?
- Did recruited teachers attend the professional development sessions? During the sessions, were teachers engaged and on task?
- Was feedback on the efficacy of the sessions gathered? Did this feedback specifically address the contribution made by faculty?

- Was information from the feedback received and
  other inputs such as observations of implementation used to
  assess (and, if necessary, refine) the professional development?

As evaluation development continues, a similar process is
followed for the other sets of activities portrayed in the logic
model: recruitment, engaging faculty, coaching, and provision of
supplemental instruction. Although the resultant list is long and
comprehensive, the evaluator realizes that it is incomplete. Specifically, looking at each activity alone is not an accurate reflection
of the logic model. A critical aspect of the theory of change relates
to the relationship among three of the components: professional
development, supplemental program implementation, and faculty engagement. They are not expected to act independently; as
the logic model shows, they are expected to complement each
other and become integrated. This expectation leads to additional
questions that directly examine the relationship among the parts:

- To what extent and in what ways do higher education faculty
  contribute to development of the professional development
  component? How were faculty involved in actual delivery of
  instruction? What worked well about the partnership, and
  which aspects could use further support?
- Did the professional development sessions include coverage
  of instruction in both the regular and the supplemental
  programs? Do teachers feel the professional development
  program showed how regular and supplemental instruction
  could be coordinated and complementary?

Progress Evaluation

A similar approach could be taken in beginning to list questions
of relevance to examining progress toward goals. Here the outcome section of the logic model gives guidance to the evaluator
(Figure 7.3).

For example, if we consider the outcome of "increased use of
inquiry-based instructional strategies," some progress questions
suggest themselves:

FIGURE 7.3. USING OUTCOMES TO DEFINE A STARTING POINT
FOR FORMATIVE EVALUATION.

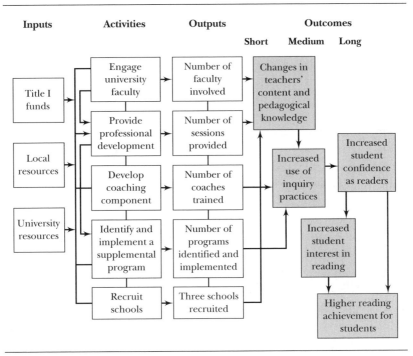

- Are teachers increasing their use of small group instruction?
- Are teachers using an appropriate mix of teacher-led and student-led strategies?
- Are teachers balancing the need for direct instruction with more open-ended strategies?
- Are teachers effectively combining the supplemental program with the regular program?
- Are teachers using graphics and other visuals to help reinforce critical concepts?

SUMMATIVE EVALUATION

The logic model shows us that there are five critical outcomes summative evaluation needs to address—two that involve teachers and three that relate more closely to students. They are changes in teacher knowledge, increased use of inquiry practice on the part of teachers, increased student achievement, students' increased confidence in self as a reader, and students' increased interest in reading. Our discussion of using the logic model to scaffold evaluation focuses on the three student outcomes.

Looking at the long-term outcomes, the basic questions are these:

- Does achievement increase for participating students?
- Do participating students show increased confidence in themselves as readers?
- Do participating students have increased interest in reading?

The logic model clearly shows what the long-term goals of the project are and which areas need to be addressed to determine whether the program is a success. It is important to recognize, however, that the logic model does not yield all the information that is needed for a summative evaluation. As with formative evaluation, the questions that the logic model brings to the fore are a starting point, not an end point for evaluation thinking. Indeed, discussion of the questions that emerge from the logic model frequently raises additional issues and may even result in changes being made to the logic model and the project.

As an illustration, let's look more closely at the question of whether achievement increases. Once the question of increased student achievement is identified, several additional matters must be addressed. First, exactly what does "achievement" mean to the program developers? Second, the project must define what kinds of outcomes will in fact constitute credible evidence of program effectiveness. Third, appropriate instruments or approaches for measuring the outcomes must be determined. As with the formative evaluation questions just discussed, the logic model leads to development of what might be called first-level questions that outline an evaluation plan. As with most outlines, however, new issues arise as it is filled in.

In the example we are discussing, once the question of impact on achievement is identified, exactly what this means needs to be clarified. This may be a task for the evaluator, or one best carried out as a broader group discussion. In the current example, the evaluator did not feel she had sufficient knowledge to take the next steps by herself. Instead, she and the project staff had to spend some time discussing what achievement means in the project and how it should be measured. Not surprisingly, such discussion led to emergence of "test performance" (the definition of achievement), and particularly "increases in passing rates on high stakes proficiency tests" (the evidence and the instrument), as being of high priority. This definition of achievement made the criterion for success clearer, but subsequent discussion indicated that it was incomplete. Ultimately, the evaluator and the project staff identified a series of questions about achievement that the evaluation should address:

- Did students increase their proficiency scores on tests of English language arts and reading?
- Did increases occur across all skill areas, or were some areas affected more strongly than others?
- Did all student groups profit from the intervention? How effective was the instruction for struggling readers? for ELL students? for students who were and were not receiving free or reduced-price lunch? for students from various racial ethnic groups?

Defining achievement always poses some challenges in educational evaluation, but even more challenges emerge when other areas are considered. Consider the second question identified in the logic model ("Did the students increase confidence in self as a reader?"). Indeed, this outcome, like many others that evaluators must address, is one that seems on the surface to be clear but becomes less so when closely examined from an evaluation perspective. In the present case, taking the next step and asking the question of what behaviors would be expected if the project is successful revealed that stakeholders had quite diverse definitions of what would amount to evidence of success.

What are some possible ways of addressing whether or not a person is confident in skills as a reader? In this case, some of the project team members suggested that expression of liking to read would show confidence. Others suggested that it was important to find out whether the students felt they could understand what they read. A variant on this is being able to understand what is communicated through various types of writing—technical, writing, stories or narratives, newspapers, and so on. Others offered up the caveat that even proficient readers sometimes cannot understand what is written—in a technical manual, for instance. The discussion then turned to consideration of whether confidence should be broken down into confidence in reading various kinds of written materials, with each explored separately. If that was the case, it appeared that the logic model should be slightly revised to call attention to the necessity for reading instruction across various types of materials and perhaps assessing teachers' ability to instruct across forms and formats. This notion caused some to question the professional development being provided and the coverage of the supplemental program they had selected. After considerable debate, the suggestion was made that confidence per se wasn't what they were interested in and that addressing confidence wasn't central to the theory of change under which they were working. They decided that the key outcome was "interest in reading" and would eliminate the area of confidence.

PRIORITIZING EVALUATION QUESTIONS FOR THE EVALUATION

Once questions are delineated, the next step is prioritizing which opportunities will be addressed and which set aside. There are several factors that have an impact on what is selected for evaluation. The first is the importance of the factor to the theory of change. Not all components of the logic model are seen as equally important. Working together with the project team, the evaluator must review the opportunities to determine which ones are central to confirming or disconfirming the theory and which are not. Other things being equal, the features that are most critical to the theory of change should be given the highest priority.

Nevertheless, even prioritizing in this way may leave the evaluator with too full a plate to handle; there are several other criteria to be considered. First, one set of issues relates to feasibility. Are there tools available for measuring the selected features, or do new tools have to be developed? If new tools are needed, what is the cost—in terms of time and money—of developing valid and reliable measurement instruments? A related issue is whether the evaluation team has the skills to undertake the development task. Second, there is the question of need. Is the feature one that has received considerable study before, or does it have a less established research basis? If not all areas can be addressed, it may be strategic to focus on those that have the potential to break new ground, rather than ones for which previous findings are being replicated.

Third, there are practical issues. What is the utility of finding out about the feature? Can the questions be expected to yield information that is actionable (that is, the data will generate information that can be acted on, such that the area is in the control of the project team members)? Also, if the feature of interest is an outcome, can it be expected to occur within the time frame allotted for the study? High-priority outcomes are frequently those that are long-term and beyond the reach of most initial evaluation efforts. Fourth, there are political issues to keep in mind. Who has an interest in finding the answer to the question? How important is the question to critical stakeholders and gatekeepers?

SUMMARY

The logic model supplies a framework for identifying formative and summative evaluation questions. By looking at activities and outcomes, it is possible to develop a comprehensive list of questions that could be addressed. Once a comprehensive list is developed, questions need to be prioritized. Many criteria contribute to the prioritization process; in most cases, technical, practical, and political concerns all play a role.

QUESTIONS TO CONSIDER

1. Take another activity shown in the logic model and enumerate the possible formative evaluation questions.
2. Discuss how you would prioritize the evaluation questions, and explain your rationale.

CHAPTER EIGHT

USING A LOGIC MODEL TO SUPPORT EXPLANATORY EVALUATION

The previous chapter showed how the logic model can be a way of identifying formative and summative evaluation questions. The purpose of this chapter is to show how evaluation can go beyond responding to formative and summative evaluation questions and contribute to research literature. We discuss how the logic model guides the evaluator in assessing the theory of change and the contributions that can be made to our knowledge of what works and what doesn't.

EVALUATION AS A TOOL FOR DEEPENING OUR UNDERSTANDING

In Chapter One, we discussed the evaluation philosophy called "program theory" and suggested that logic modeling and program theory are closely related. Program theory is a way of making explicit the assumptions underlying an intervention. It describes the causal linkages that are assumed to occur from project start to goal attainment; it clearly defines the theory of change underlying a program or policy. The logic model amounts to a way of portraying such theories concretely and visually.

In Chapter Seven, we showed how the logic model can be used to guide formative and summative evaluation. Specifically, we illustrated how the activities and outcomes depicted in the logic model can help define the questions that are asked as the project is implemented (formative evaluation) and is completed (summative evaluation).

To many, defining those questions and determining how to measure them complete the evaluation development task. Indeed, discussion that attempts to spell out the difference between research and evaluation may stress the point that the role of evaluation is to address the extent to which activities happened or outcomes were attained. Research, in contrast, has the responsibility for explaining why something occurs, or addressing theory, contributing to what is traditionally called the research base.

Evaluators who espouse logic modeling frequently reject this distinction and feel that evaluation has three parts, not two. In addition to formative and summative evaluation, users of the logic model feel that the responsibility of the evaluator is also to conduct *explanatory evaluation,* which has as its objective assessing why something works (or doesn't work); it includes developing an understanding of the *why* and *under what conditions* in addition to examining whether or not goals have been achieved. For evaluators who assume this responsibility, the logic model scaffolds a broader kind of evaluation study than that illustrated in the previous chapter.

Using the Logic Model to Assess the Theory of Change

Presented in Figure 8.1 is the logic model that eventually evolved from the considerations described in Chapter Seven.

Many questions about implementation of the project and its outcomes evolved from examination of this model. However, missing from our earlier discussion and the resultant evaluation plan was attention to the underlying theory on which the project was built, the linkages showing interaction among activities, and the chain of activities expected to lead to the outcomes desired. Those who see logic modeling as an alternative to experimental design suggest that confirming the underlying theory takes us a step closer to being able to claim causality.

FIGURE 8.1. LOGIC MODEL.

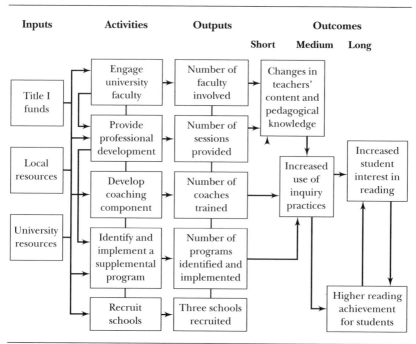

From the description presented in Chapter Seven, we can see that the project rests on a theory of change that posits:

1. The importance of content knowledge and the special role of university faculty in imparting this knowledge
2. The need for multiple supports— (professional development, coaching in both content and pedagogy, a supplemental program)
3. An assumption that change in teacher knowledge leads to change in practice, which ultimately leads to changes in student learning and behavior
4. Changes in student achievement and interest in reading occurring at approximately the same time

An evaluation that is framed as an explanatory evaluation must also examine these four assumptions and then determine if they were implemented and sequenced as intended, to acquire an understanding of the extent to which the underlying theory can be supported. That is, to support a causal interpretation it would be necessary to show:

- Content-rich professional development was furnished, and the faculty had a significant role in its development and delivery.
- Teachers received appropriate training in the regular and supplemental programs; coaching was ongoing and timely in supporting and extending this training.
- Teachers participating in the professional development showed increased knowledge of content and pedagogy.
- Increased knowledge was followed by changes in practice, in both the regular and the supplemental programs.
- Students of teachers who participated in professional development and showed these changes had a gain in achievement, as well as increased interest in reading.

In other words, the evaluator needs to ask: Has a chain of evidence been established? Does this chain of evidence support the theory underlying the program?

Let's start with the first assumption—"the importance of content knowledge and the special role of university faculty in providing the knowledge". To assess this assumption, what are some of the additional questions that an evaluation will have to address?

An initial question could examine the extent to which providing content knowledge appears to be a critical part of the professional development program, as well as the role played by faculty in creating and making available this content knowledge.

- To what extent does the professional development give accurate, in-depth content knowledge to the participants?
- Is there evidence that higher education faculty have made a significant contribution to developing this aspect of the professional development?
- Were faculty involved in actually delivering instruction?
- What worked well about the partnership between the faculty and the K–12 staff? What aspects could use further refinement?

The second assumption—the need for multiple supports—can be addressed similarly. Because of the likely variation that occurs in delivering interventions, if implementation is well documented it may be possible to examine what results when this assumption is or is not met. That is, the evaluator could try to systematically examine cases where varying combinations of support were in place to see the patterns of outcomes that emerge.

Explanatory evaluation would consider certain questions:

- Did the professional development sessions include coverage of instruction in both the regular and the supplemental programs? Did the teachers feel that the professional development program furnished adequate information on content, use of inquiry-based practices, and the specific regular and supplemental programs that were to be used?
- Were the coaches knowledgeable about content and pedagogy? Were they familiar with the specific features of the regular and supplemental programs?
- Did they make available the expected amount of coaching to teachers during the school year?
- Are any differences found in resultant teacher behavior where the sessions were perceived to be poorly coordinated, coaches were not sufficiently knowledgeable, or coaching was limited and not timely?

Turning to the next step, the evaluator would pose some additional questions about the impact on teachers and teaching:

- Did teachers who participated in the professional development show increased knowledge of content and pedagogical practice?
- Did teachers who participated in the professional development show changes in their teaching practices aligned with what was taught in the professional development sessions?
- Did acquisition of new knowledge precede and predict the extent to which changes in actual teaching practices emerged?
- Were these changes uniform, or did they vary systematically as a function of teacher background and experience?

Finally, let's look at the ultimate outcome area, student achievement. Possible questions:

- Was there a relationship between change in teaching practice and change in student achievement or interest?
- Were there any differences in these student outcomes related to differences in the teachers' professional development experiences?
- Did extent or quality of coaching appear to have any impact?
- Did changes occur in both achievement and interest in reading? Did changes occur simultaneously in these two outcome areas, or was there any consistent pattern of differential emergence?

Depending on the pattern of *yes* and *no* answers to these questions, in combination with what the summative findings show, the evaluator can build an assessment of which parts of the theory of change are supported, which do not seem to hold up, and where the data suggest that the theory is questionable. The findings from the series of questions allow the evaluator and the project team to revisit the logic model and refine it, on the basis of patterns and sequences that are or are not confirmed.

For example, let's assume that overall the project appears to lead to positive outcomes. According to the summative evaluation findings, the results show that overall the students increased achievement and interest in reading. The change was uneven, though, and in some cases students made far greater gains than others. Further, student achievement and student interest in reading did not always change as expected; there were a number of cases in which achievement changed but interest did not. Where changes did occur in both outcome measures, change in achievement generally occurred before change in interest.

What does this set of findings imply with regard to the theory of change? To answer this question we must look at what the evaluation found out about the four assumptions. Returning to the questions laid out earlier, suppose the evaluation shows that with regard to the activities:

- Higher education faculty did take major responsibility for developing the content portion of the professional development; and the professional development did provide accurate, in-depth content knowledge for the participants.

- Faculty did deliver the instruction regarding content during the professional development sessions. Teachers indicated that they found this part of the training especially useful and that they felt they learned much more than in professional development sessions previously attended.
- The professional development sessions were uneven with regard to coverage of the regular and supplemental programs. There did not seem to be enough time to cover content, the theory and practice of inquiry-based instruction, and the specific features of both programs.
- Coaching was provided, but in a number of cases the coaches were not knowledgeable about the supplemental program. Further, they were able to help teachers in the area of inquiry-based instruction but were quite uneven in their content knowledge. The amount of coaching also varied widely and generally was less than expected.

Turning now to changes in teachers and teaching:

- The data showed that teachers made significant gains in their content knowledge; changes were greater for new teachers than for veterans.
- Changes in use of inquiry also occurred, but not across the board. It appeared that these changes occurred independently of those in content knowledge. More experienced teachers were somewhat less likely to change their practice than newer teachers were.
- The teachers who made the greatest changes in their use of inquiry-based practices were also the ones who reported being most satisfied with the extent to which the professional development offered coordinated information about the supplemental and regular programs.
- Coaching appeared to have a large impact on use of inquiry, especially for less-experienced teachers. Even for teachers who felt their professional development did not do a good job of supplying coordinated information, significant progress was made. However, hours of coaching did not relate systematically to changes in this area.

Regarding student outcomes:

- There was a strong and significant relationship between changes in teachers' content knowledge and in student achievement.
- Change in use of inquiry-based practices was also significantly related to change in achievement for the newer teachers.
- For the veteran teachers, change in content knowledge was related to change in achievement for the higher achieving students, but not for the struggling readers—the main target of the program.
- Changes in content knowledge and inquiry-based practices were not related to changes in interest in reading. Change in this variable seemed to develop slowly and not be systematically related to major program variables.

What do these findings mean for the project's theory of change? Here are a few of the more salient findings.

- The findings suggest that teacher experience is a variable that needs to be looked at more closely. The relationships among variables differed for new and veteran teachers, as did the impact of the program on their students. Overall the project appears to be a success, but closer examination indicates that veteran teachers require different supports from what new teachers need. The theory of change does not work in the same way for both groups.
- The findings do not support the initial assumption that change in content knowledge would lead to change in use of inquiry-based practices. Although both kinds of change occurred, they did so independently.
- The treatment did not result in changes in student interest in reading. Some changes did occur for some students, but this outcome variable did not seem to be related systematically to any of the variables that the project addressed.

The findings also raised some questions about the nature of the treatment and its implementation; this requires further examination. On the one hand, there was some evidence that professional development addressing both supplemental and regular instruction well led to the desired changes in teacher practices, the importance of this component was unclear because it was implemented effectively in only a few cases. Coaching seemed able to overcome inadequate professional development in this area, even if the coaches were not completely familiar with the supplemental program. However, amount of coaching did not seem to make a systematic difference; how and why coaching worked was unclear.

Figure 8.2 shows the beginning of a revised logic model that incorporates some of these findings. Interest in reading is eliminated as an outcome; change in teacher content knowledge and increased use of inquiry-based practices are not dependent on one another, and each has an impact on achievement; coaching, professional development, and the supplemental program are highlighted to show that these areas need further examination; and the whole model is changed to apply only to new teachers.

FIGURE 8.2. REVISED LOGIC MODEL: NEW TEACHERS ONLY.

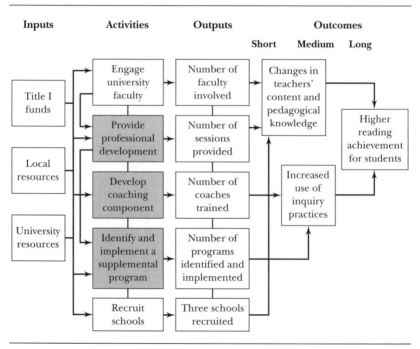

It is clear that new investigations will have to be undertaken before the effectiveness of this intervention plan can be confirmed or rejected. One thing this first stage of explanatory evaluation has confirmed is that partnership between university faculty and the K–12 educators can be developed and implemented to support instruction. Also, the professional development program as delivered did help new teachers change their teaching practices and assist struggling students in improving their achievement.

As the development and testing of the program continues, the theory of change will clearly undergo a number of modifications. In addition, it is likely that these modifications will include addition of new variables. It is always important to remember to remain open to examining whether factors other than those originally included could have played a role in determining the pattern of relationships and outcomes that emerged. Did any other factors—factors not initially part of the underlying theory—seem to have a systematic and important impact on the changes that were found? One danger with the logic model is that looking only for things specified in the model can lead the evaluator to miss other variables playing an important role.

SUMMARY

This chapter shows how the evaluator can use the logic model to go beyond examining formative and summative issues, to actually assessing the validity of the theory of change. Building on the questions enumerated in the previous chapter, the evaluator who is engaged in explanatory evaluation examines whether the contingencies and sequence posited in the model are confirmed or disconfirmed by the empirical findings. The end result is typically a revision of the theory of change and identification of questions that need to be more fully explored. Explanatory evaluation can make a major contribution to our understanding of what works and what does not.

QUESTIONS TO CONSIDER

1. Discuss the pros and cons of doing explanatory evaluation. Under what conditions is it important? How might it affect the

interaction between the evaluators and the project development team?

2. Consider the model developed for new teachers. If you were taking the next step in the evaluation, how would you further explore the coaching and supplementary program components? Draw logic models that suggest alternative theories of change worth exploring.

3. Remember the original formulation of the project that included both confidence in self as a reader and interest in reading as medium-term outcomes. Think of how a study might reexamine their influences. Show the logic models that would depict the theories of change.

CHAPTER NINE

CHALLENGES IN DEVELOPING
LOGIC MODELS

This chapter discusses some of the common problems encountered in developing and using logic models. Some we have noted in earlier chapters as we laid out the underlying basis for logic models; others are new. The discussion is organized around several clusters of issues that range widely. Specifically, we discuss:

- Misunderstanding of the basic features of the logic model
- Finding the right grain size
- Seeing the logic model as a silver bullet
- Maintaining objectivity

This discussion of problems is not meant to discourage you from using logic models, but rather to sensitize you to challenges that may be encountered as the tool is employed.

MISUNDERSTANDING OF THE BASIC
FEATURES OF THE LOGIC MODEL

Logic models can be difficult to develop and almost impossible to use if the basic features and properties of a logic model are not well understood. There are four common failings that occur with some frequency in this arena: confusing terms, substituting specific measures for more general outcomes, assuming unidirectionality, and failing to specify a time frame for activities.

Confusing Terms

Perhaps the biggest stumbling block for people new to using logic models is distinguishing an outcome from an activity or output. Let's review and expand on the definition of these three components.

An *outcome* is a change, usually in a person, group of persons, or institutional structure, that is reflective of the goal the project is trying to achieve.

An *activity* is the action or series of actions undertaken to move toward the goal. In terms of process and product thinking, the outcome is the product and the action is the process. The value of the action is that it leads to the product. It is instrumental in reaching the goal, but it is not the goal itself.

An *output* is some measure reflecting that an action has taken place. It is the immediate result of the action. It does not reflect attainment of a project goal, but it does help to document that actions have been taken that are expected to lead to the goal. Typically, an output is expressed as some kind of a number.

All too often, outputs and activities are mistaken for outcomes. There are probably several reasons. First, project developers are accustomed to thinking in terms of action. They are constantly in the position of developing and implementing activities, and making sure the activities occur in a timely fashion. They are process-focused. It is not surprising, therefore, that carrying out a process effectively becomes an end in and of itself. Second, it is easier to confirm that a process has been carried out than to affirm an outcome. The sometimes extended duration required in achieving outcomes can be frustrating, leading those engaged in an intervention to celebrate successful achievement of an activity. An output offering evidence that an activity has been undertaken is accepted as an indicator that a goal has been reached. Third, though the reasons already discussed assume that both activities and goals have been defined, in other cases the goal is actually lost. The activity or process becomes the goal and the instrumental utility of the activity is never addressed. Fourth, to make the situation even more complicated, in some projects these distinctions are moot because the goal is actually implementation of a process. This is where the confusion really grows thick. When a particular project is embedded in a developmental chain or series of projects, the end "goal" of any segment may in fact be to develop, try out, and fine-tune an activity or create an output. In such a case, even though it may be meaningful to develop a logic model that shows how all the segments fit together toward the more distal goal, for project evaluation purposes such a model is not useful. The logic model for such a project will have as its "outcome" successful implementation of the activity.

SUBSTITUTING SPECIFIC MEASURES FOR MORE GENERAL OUTCOMES

The most appropriate progression in developing a logic model is to identify an outcome area, operationalize it, and then identify an appropriate measure for assessing the area. For example, achievement might be the outcome area, performance on a standardized test the operationalization, and the TerraNova achievement test as the particular instrument for measuring the outcome. Sometimes project staff may have difficulty separating an outcome area from a specific measure or instrument. That is, instead of articulating achievement as the outcome, staff may want to identify an instrument—here, for instance, the TerraNova—as the outcome of interest. This may be appropriate if TerraNova scores are really all that the project is interested in, but narrowing down outcomes in this way is more often than not too limiting. Whenever possible, it is better to identify a general area, examine alternative definitions of the area, and then suggest one or two measures of the area that might capture the desired information.

ASSUMING UNIDIRECTIONALITY

The classic depiction of a logic model with inputs on the far left side, outcomes on the far right, and right-pointing arrows connecting the components can create another set of problems. This visual display, along with English speakers' ingrained left-to-right scanning of words in written text, almost compels the user to think of a logic model as something that must be in a left-to-right progression.

That this is not the case is frequently very difficult (but very important) to understand. Neither the evaluator nor the project developer will be able to use the logic model effectively without being disabused of this notion. Assuming unidirectionality is a problem for at least two major reasons. First, the left-to-right assumption fails to take into account the interactions and feedback loops that are part of most functioning logic models, if not all of them. In only the simplest projects of limited duration it is true that what happens at the short-term outcome stage can be expected to have an impact on the activities component. The effect may be small or large. That is, information from short-term outcomes may lead to refinement of a set of activities, or it may require reformulation of the focus, scope, or sequence of actions. Similarly, what happens at the long-term outcome stage can be expected to influence the next project, if not the next step in the current project. Second, an assumption of unidirectionality may appear to create the undesirable circumstance that it is the inputs driving the project, rather than the goals and specific outcomes that are expected to be attained. In our examples of logic model development, we consistently begin with the outcomes and then work backward and forward through the various components as the logic model is created. Working both back and forth and up and down is a central part of modeling. It is for this reason that some people prefer logic models resembling webs rather than the linear depiction we use here. The web format is useful in this way, although webbing may make it more difficult to determine what is expected to lead to what.

FAILING TO SPECIFY A TIME FRAME

A logic model is not complete until some notion of time is added to the theory of action that is depicted. For implementation and evaluation purposes, it is important to have some idea of when one can expect activities to be completed and outcomes of varying degrees of completeness. For convenience sake, short-term outcomes are generally expected to occur within two years, intermediate outcomes within two to five years, and long-term outcomes after five years. However, defining outcomes in this way is like using the mean value to describe what is happening in a population with a large distribution. It gives an idea of where things stand, but it really does not represent the reality of what is happening at all accurately. The case is similar regarding specification of time frames for outcomes and activities in developing logic models. The particular nature of the project, rather than generic rules or frameworks, must drive the time frame.

The problem has important ramifications. If the time frame is not explicitly addressed (or is addressed imprecisely), evaluators may look for an outcome too soon and erroneously conclude that the theory of action was incorrect even though this is not the case. Conversely, under these circumstances the alternative may also happen: too much time may be allowed to pass before it is decided that objectives are not being met and that the theory of change needs to be revisited. Even in fairly simple projects, predicting when a result might be found can be a challenge. In more complex projects, involving multiple entities and a variety of outcomes, the challenge is considerable. Again, here as in other areas it is important to remember that the logic model is not set in concrete. Time frames can be modified on the basis of what is learned as the project unfolds. An educated guess may be the best that one can hope for under some situations, but a guess is far better than failing to specify when implementation will be completed and change might be expected.

FINDING THE RIGHT GRAIN SIZE

Another challenge is figuring out the appropriate level of detail to put into the logic model.

GETTING LOST IN COMPLEXITY

For simple projects such as adopting a new protocol to identify students who may be at risk, developing a logic model may be a relatively straightforward activity. However, in some cases—especially where the project involves several components and is expected to address multiple outcome areas—development of a logic model can become complex, time-consuming, and frustrating. The challenge is finding the right grain size, the right level at which to describe the project's theory of change without leaving out critical components or including too many details.

OVERSIMPLIFYING

Of course, the converse of getting lost in complexity is failing to be sufficiently clear about the components of a logic model and what is expected to lead to what. This is a significant problem when separate activities are lumped together and linkages fail to produce much differentiation in how specific activities, outputs, and outcomes might be linked. In such a case, the logic model may be an easily accessible visual that shows the major parts of a project. But the model fails miserably as a depiction of the underlying theory and a scaffolding for evaluation.

SEEING THE LOGIC MODEL AS A SILVER BULLET

With the increasing popularity of logic models in the field of evaluation, a new danger has arisen: seeing the logic model as some kind of cure-all that ensures the success of both the project and the evaluation. A logic model is only a tool. Its efficacy depends on the quality of the materials it has to work on. If the materials are faulty, application of the tool will not change the basic inadequacy of the design. There are several common mistakes in this area:

- Trying to create a logic model when no real theory of change exists
- Failing to recognize and explore alternative theories of change
- Failing to be sensitive to factors outside the logic model
- Believing a logic model obviates the need for rigorous design

TRYING TO CREATE A LOGIC MODEL WHEN NO REAL THEORY OF CHANGE EXISTS

In Chapter One two types of sources of knowledge were identified as being important for developing a theory of change: research and experience. The theory of change builds on what has been learned from previous knowledge-gathering events and may attempt to replicate or expand to a new situation what was found. There are expectations about which activities should lead to which outcomes, and that the purpose of the project is to confirm or disconfirm these expectations. Not all projects follow this particular knowledge-building approach, however. Sometimes a project is initiated to see what happens, or to try out a new technology in a different situation. There is also a well-respected line of work built on the notion that exploration of ideas should be "goal free." In such cases, attempting to build a logic model can be inappropriate or even counterproductive.

FAILING TO RECOGNIZE AND EXPLORE ALTERNATIVE THEORIES OF CHANGE

It is also the case that building a logic model does not necessarily mean the logic model being created appropriately sums up the critical features that need to be considered. One strong criticism of logic models is that they can focus on one possible theory of change without devoting sufficient attention to competing theories that should also be recognized. It is important to try to tease out these alternative theories and recognize where they may suggest other hypotheses to explore, if at all possible. A real danger is that a focus on a single theory of change may not accommodate appropriate sensitivity to events or outcomes that fall outside the logic model's focus. If the result of the logic model is to blind the evaluator to influences or outcomes that fall outside the model, the work is ill served.

FAILING TO BE SENSITIVE TO FACTORS OUTSIDE THE LOGIC MODEL

Third, in creating the logic model contextual features may be given short shrift. It is appropriate that the focus of the model rests on the components and the linkages. However, the model can be incomplete and inaccurate if important contextual features are not also spelled out. In the initial chapter, in which the idea of the logic model was introduced, we pointed out the contribution of systems theory. No intervention exists in isolation. Interventions are always carried out within a large system or systems. Specifying the critical features of these systems is important to the knowledge-building process and to scaffolding generalization from specific examples to a wider universe.

Believing a Logic Model Obviates the Need for a Rigorous Design

The logic model offers a way of making explicit the critical features of a project and how its components are expected to lead to some desired outcomes. Confidence in the accuracy of the theory follows from implementation of the model resulting in the expected outcomes. The approach is useful in situations in which it is not possible to create alternative interventions against which the success of the treatment can be compared, or in which the value of new theories is initially being explored. But validation by logic model is generally not considered to be as rigorous a proof as what is achieved through a study design employing experimental or quasi-experimental methodologies. In fact, developing alternative logic models and then testing their relative efficacy through experimental means may really be more of a gold standard than the much-touted randomized experiment. Whenever possible, an evaluation can be strengthened by combining the advantages of logic modeling with experimental design. In reality, though, such opportunities are likely to be infrequent and costly.

Maintaining Objectivity

Finally, it is important as an evaluator to thoroughly understand what a project is about, while at the same time maintaining objectivity and remaining a certain distance from decisions about what the shape and scope of a project will be. The logic model can be a two-edged sword where objectivity is concerned. On the one hand, the modeling activity gives the evaluator greater understanding of the project and higher sensitivity to what needs to be measured and when. On the other hand, the engagement and interaction that frequently evolve as the evaluator works with the project team to develop a logic model may pose a threat to this objectivity. In development of a logic model, it is not unusual for the evaluator to take on the role of what has been called a critical friend. The evaluator in this role works with the team to clarify assumptions and expectations, resolve differences of opinion, and in many cases fine-tune the project's plan. A delicate balance must be maintained between raising questions because what is said truly is not clear or does not seem to hold together and raising questions that stem at least in part from the evaluator's own beliefs about what research says about how a particular phenomenon should be addressed. To the extent that the questions raised by the evaluator inappropriately influence what the project becomes, the evaluator creates a situation in which he or she may be more invested in affirming the theory of change than might be desirable.

There is no simple way of dealing with this threat. Each situation brings its own set of challenges to maintaining objectivity. It is important that the evaluator remain sensitive to this issue and recognize the difference between sharpening the theory of change and shaping it.

Summary

In this chapter, we reviewed some of the common challenges in developing logic models. The challenges relate to development of a valid and useful model, how the model is used, and the role of the evaluator. There is no one way to overcome these challenges; each must be addressed within the bounds of the project and evaluation task. The important thing is to remain sensitive to the issues and resolve them in ways that maximize each individual situation.

Questions to Consider

1. Goal-free evaluation is cited as one situation in which a logic model is not appropriate. Can you think of any other evaluation paradigms that might be incompatible with using a logic model? Why might this be so?

2. Sometimes an activity or process, rather than a change in an outcome area, is the goal of a project. Think of some cases in which this might be so. What would the logic models look like?

3. Review the strengths of the logic model and its limitations. What makes the tool most useful? Where might it be less useful?

CHAPTER TEN

DEVELOPING LOGIC MODELS FOR COMPLEX PROJECTS

In this chapter and the next, we look closely at the use of logic models for a variety of evaluation purposes. Building on the issues that were raised in the preceding chapters, we share some case studies of logic model development and use, and the challenges encountered.

The present chapter looks at the Reading First Program and discusses a variety of ways in which logic models can be used in evaluating complex projects. Specifically, the example:

- Shows how logic models can help clarify evaluation issues in complex projects
- Shows how logic models can address the levels and components of a complex project
- Reminds us that logic models are tools and not answers

THE CONTEXT OF THE EVALUATION

Reading First (RF) is a major national program aimed at increasing literacy at the K–3 grade levels. It provides funds to states—on the basis of an accepted state proposal—that in turn furnish funds to districts and schools within districts. Eligible schools are ones that are the most needy, defined in terms of socioeconomic status and test scores in reading. Reading First builds on what is known about effective approaches to early reading instruction, emphasizing the importance of addressing five essential features: phonics, phonemic awareness, vocabulary, fluency, and comprehension.

The program includes professional development, technical assistance, adoption of appropriate research-based materials, and extra staffing at the school level. Although the federal program lays out the basic parameters of what is required, within these parameters states are able to structure their own programs, keeping in mind their particular context, resources, and related efforts.

The major goal of Reading First is to increase the literacy of students in grades K–3, ensuring that students from all groups attain the highest level of performance possible. In addition, it is expected that the program will have an impact on teachers and principals, increasing their understanding of scientifically based reading and their ability to offer instruction aligned with research findings. The program is also seen as a capacity-building effort, one expected to change the infrastructure that supports early literacy instruction and leaves behind an educational system better prepared to serve all students across the nation.

The Evaluation Challenge

State A has been awarded a grant from the federal Department of Education to implement RF. The program "Reading First State A" (RFSA) is designed to meet the goals outlined by the department, while at the same time building on the literacy infrastructure already established in the state. This infrastructure includes a set of standards for English language arts, a relationship with professional development providers at various universities, and a technical assistance framework based on regional delivery of support services. The state is requesting an evaluation that:

- Examines the extent to which the program is meeting the goal of enhancing student literacy
- Assesses how consistent RFSA is with other state initiatives and established standards
- Informs what works and what does not in terms of meeting the instructional goals
- Evaluates the management strategy used and the lessons learned for other major reform efforts

At the time of initiation of the request for proposals, RFSA is already under way. A request for proposals from districts was issued and the first cohort of grantees announced and funded. Three cohorts are expected. Initial plans have been developed and implemented for professional development and technical assistance.

Challenge One: Clarifying Evaluation Purposes

The first challenge faced by the evaluator is clarifying what the state wants to know about the RFSA program. Examination of the four evaluation requests from the state reveals that the evaluation is expected to serve multiple purposes:

- There is the summative question of whether or not student literacy improves.
- There is a more systemic question of how the RFSA program aligns with other state programs (and, implied, the consequences of alignment or lack of alignment).
- There is the issue of developing deeper understanding of the dynamics of the change process and the factors that affect it. The state wants to go beyond knowing if it has succeeded (or not) to understanding why, and the factors that contribute to or inhibit attainment of its goals.
- State A is interested in furthering its understanding of how to effectively manage a program of this scope and complexity. There is a desire to learn more about management and organizational change, as well as instructional improvement.

This array of questions appears to be looking at the program, and the same features of the program, through at least two lenses. The first is the lens of education, assessing whether or not instructional goals are attained. The second is the lens of program management, assessing whether or not project oversight and management function appropriately. It seems at first that the two sets of needs can be accommodated by simply taking each feature and asking two sets of questions about it—instructional and managerial.

However, approaching the evaluation this way results in fragmenting the analysis such that the pieces of the program become the focus. What starts out as a systemic approach to change loses its systemic quality. In the face of this, the evaluation is reconceptualized into two substudies: (1) a study of instruction and learning and (2) a study of management. Two logic models are developed, one addressing the instructional issues and a second dealing with the management and organizational change issues.

Figure 10.1 shows the beginning of a logic model that focuses on changes in instruction and learning. Figure 10.2 shows the logic model that addresses management and organizational issues. It is clear that even though both address the same features—professional development, technical assistance, testing, and so forth—the goals for the two studies are quite different, as are their underlying theories of change. The logic models make clearer some of the

FIGURE 10.1. RFSA LOGIC MODEL FOR INSTRUCTION AND LEARNING.

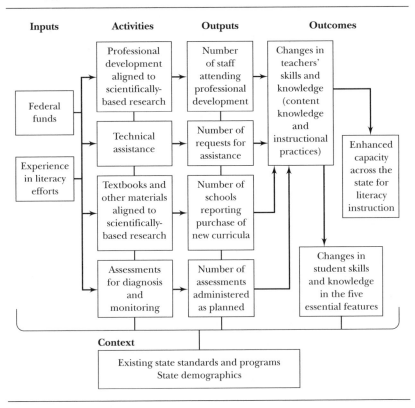

distinctions required. Very different evaluation plans and types of
data are needed to address the two sets of issues.

Challenge Two: Defining the Boundaries
of the Investigation

The second challenge is to define the boundaries of the evaluation. In Chapter One we discussed systems and the idea that

FIGURE 10.2. RFSA LOGIC MODEL FOR MANAGEMENT
AND ORGANIZATIONAL CHANGE.

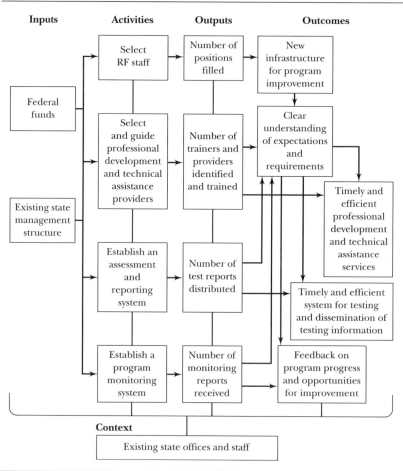

a system may be composed of multiple subsystems. A complex reform program such as Reading First can be thought of as a system, containing subsystems, that is nested within a larger system. Specifically:

• The Reading First Program is made up of several pieces—professional development, materials support, technical assistance, school change—each of which plays an important role in the functioning of the overall RF system of change.
• Each of these pieces is itself a subsystem, with multiple interlocking parts that may function well or poorly.
• The RFSA program and its components are also part of a larger system—the state educational system—that has in place existing curricular standards, professional development supports, and school improvement efforts.

The challenge is to determine how much the theory of change needs to integrate the existing system of services. The question is the extent to which these preexisting services are part of the process being studied or part of the context in which the project is operating. Figure 10.3 shows an alternative logic model in which the role of existing services is given more prominence. (In this depiction, the outputs have been eliminated to simplify the graphic.) This is a viable alternative to the logic model portrayed in Figure 10.1, which explicitly recognizes the reality of interacting systems.

After some debate, the alternative model is rejected. It is decided that RFSA will be considered the focus for the evaluation, with the extant and ongoing state system assuming more of a background role. The theory of change is the theory embedded in the Reading First program, and the existing state system is considered context as originally depicted.

It is important to recognize that this is not a trivial decision. The logic model depicted in Figure 10.3 clearly shows an alternative conceptualization of the variables that might be expected to affect literacy outcomes. If Figure 10.3 were adopted rather than Figure 10.1, the factors to be explored in the evaluation would be different. The same outcomes would be looked for, but the

Figure 10.3. RFSA/State Services Logic Model
for Instruction and Learning.

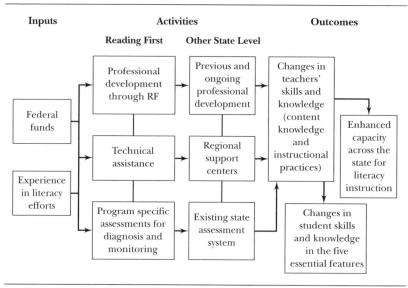

features examined in trying to explain the outcomes would be new. One criticism of using logic models that was discussed in a previous chapter is that they may cause the evaluator to ignore other plausible explanations for why change is or is not occurring. The RF example constitutes a striking illustration of the fact that more than one reasonable alternative depiction does exist and that having a logic model should not blind the evaluator to the need to be aware of alternative explanations for any result.

Challenge Three: Determining Grain Size for the Logic Model

A related issue is determining the grain size of the logic model. This is an issue we have mentioned many times in previous chapters, and one that presents a continuous challenge. Not surprisingly, the challenge is greater—and of greater consequence—in more complex projects. Figure 10.1 presents a reasonable overview of the components of the RF system and how it might be distinguished from others, but it is still at a relatively gross level of detail.

For the logic model to fully capture the theory of change and guide the evaluation, it is necessary to be more explicit about the particular features that characterize each major component. Stating that one activity is "professional development aligned to scientifically based research" is a major component that begins characterization but does not go far enough. There is a need to be more explicit about what the features are, both to (1) make sure there is shared understanding among project team members of what is meant by the term *scientifically based* and (2) define the measurable variables that will be part of the evaluation.

Let's look more closely at this professional development component. As the evaluation is planned it is important to consider who, what, and when:

FIGURE 10.4. LOGIC MODEL FOR RFSA PROFESSIONAL DEVELOPMENT—
YEAR ONE (ONE COHORT).

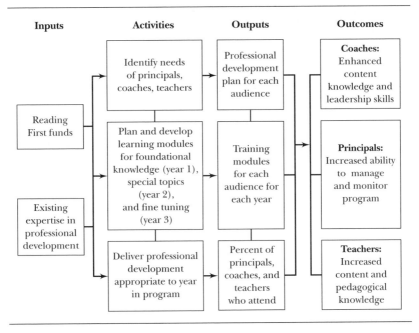

- Professional development for whom? (school-based coaches, principals, teachers, other support personnel)
- Professional development about what? (the content of instruction, working with special needs populations, pedagogy)
- Professional development at what stage of the project's evolution? (foundational knowledge for awareness, special topics for installation of practice, fine tuning for sustaining practice)

In this case, and often in complex projects, it is useful to develop a tiered logic model. The first tier (Figure 10.1) will display all the basic components, with sufficient detail to communicate the special features of the project. The second tier provides a series of minilogic models, directed at furnishing more detail for each of the component parts. Figures 10.4 and 10.5 illustrate a minimodel for professional development. They begin to lay out the steps in developing and delivering the professional development, showing the emphases expected over the three years of the

FIGURE 10.5. LOGIC MODEL FOR RFSA PROFESSIONAL DEVELOPMENT— YEAR TWO (TWO COHORTS).

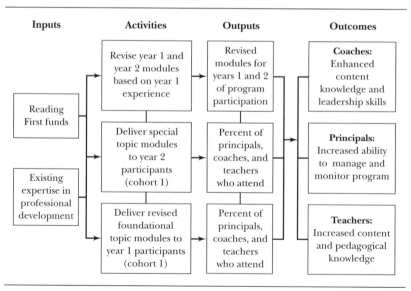

project. They also show, starting in year two, the activities that may be going on for cohorts that begin at differing times.

Challenge Four: Capturing Change over Time

There are at least two kinds of change that occur over time that are relevant to the evaluation and the logic model. The first are changes that occur in the program; they could be adding or modifying a component as new needs are identified or making component changes as other needs emerge while the project matures. In addition, because most Reading First programs fund multiple cohorts of schools, there are changes that are driven by the inconstant nature of the population. The latter can probably be effectively recognized through specifying context variables. The former has more serious implications. To the extent that unanticipated modifications to the treatment or activities must be made, it is critical to modify the project's the theory of change, and probably the evaluation plan.

For example, in RFSA there was a plan for professional development for coaches (principals and teachers) that assumed a gradual change in the focus of the professional development over the three years of RF participation. Year one is conceptualized as the year for establishing a grounding in the principles of scientifically based reading research, looking across a range of content and pedagogical issues. Year two focuses more on special topics such as working with special needs children or effectively using a variety of assessment tools to diagnose individual student needs and plan instruction. Year three is designed to both fine-tune understanding and develop a master coach who could continue to offer high-quality assistance without the support of the formal professional development structure. However, by the summer after the first year of funding it became clear that schools entering year two of the project would not necessarily be entering with the same staff that had been trained the first year. In fact, each year coaches might leave (as might teachers and principals), and there would be a mixture of trained staff and new staff with no experience in RF professional development.

Earlier chapters stressed the importance of considering the logic model to be a living thing, not a depiction established and never revisited. In the present case the logic model, and especially the minimodels for the professional development subsystem, must be revised to show the accommodations made to deal with attrition. Figure 10.6 shows the revision.

Summary

This chapter illustrates the roles that the logic model can play in complex projects. Using a single project, we illustrate ways in which logic models can be used to:

- Portray the theory of change for numerous evaluation purposes
- Make explicit the theories of change that might be applied to any one project

FIGURE 10.6. LOGIC MODEL FOR RFSA PROFESSIONAL DEVELOPMENT—
YEAR TWO REVISED (TWO COHORTS).

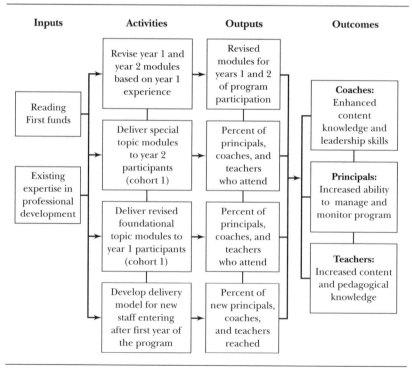

- Show the theory of change for aspects of the project
- Capture modifications in the theory of change that emerge as the project progresses

These examples continue to illustrate that a logic model is a versatile tool for clarifying and guiding evaluation projects. We are also reminded that it is a tool and not a silver bullet.

Questions to Consider

1. Using Figures 10.1 and 10.2 as scaffolding, list some formative evaluation questions that the logic models suggest. Give some examples of the data you might need to collect to address them. Identify potential areas of convergence and divergence.
2. The chapter presents two alternative logic models that could be used to scaffold evaluation of RFSA. Pick a project that you are familiar with and develop at least two alternative logic models. Explain the pros and cons of each.

Chapter Eleven

Using Logic Models to Evaluate a Family of Projects

In the previous chapter, we discussed how the logic model can be used to clarify and inform evaluation work in a complex, multipart, multiyear evaluation study. In this chapter, we present additional examples of using the logic model in other types of evaluation-related activities.

The chapter shows how the logic model can be used to:

- Create a framework for describing a family of projects
- Show variations in how projects implement the framework
- Identify the types of data that need to be gathered to explore cross-cutting hypotheses

Cross-Project Analysis

The Study of the Value-Added of IHE Engagement (VAIE) is a cross-project analysis of eight systemic reform efforts funded by the National Science Foundation's Math and Science Partnership Program. (The example here is based on work currently being conducted by Westat. Some changes to the logic model have been made in this chapter for illustrative purposes.)

The study is not a meta-analysis per se, but rather a research project that builds on other exploratory projects. The Math and Science Partnership (MSP) program is a major national research and development effort that supports innovative partnerships to improve K–12 student achievement in mathematics and science. Deep engagement of science, technology, engineering, and mathematics (STEM) disciplinary faculty at institutions of higher education (IHE) is a hallmark of this program. The program posits that disciplinary faculty can furnish the important knowledge that K–12 teachers need, and that if IHE faculty are substantially involved teachers' content knowledge and the K–12 instructional program will be strengthened. The end goal is improved student achievement.

The VAIE is a four-year study designed to integrate and build on findings that emerge from selected MSP projects developed to reach shared goals, through locally appropriate means. The cross-project study asks how STEM faculty are engaged in MSP. Does their involvement make any difference in enhancing teacher quality and increasing student achievement? Are there particular circumstances in which certain types of involvement contribute more or less than others on these dimensions? In essence, the project asks what works, for whom, and under what circumstance by way of six questions:

1. What methods (that is, strategies, practices, and policies) are being used by the projects to engage STEM faculty in their activities, and how do they differ by type of IHE?
2. What level of involvement is garnered by various methods at different types of IHE?
3. To what extent does STEM faculty involvement contribute to an increase in K–12 teacher content and pedagogical knowledge?
4. To what extent does STEM faculty involvement contribute to student achievement?
5. What are the policy implications for engaging STEM faculty?
6. How does faculty involvement evolve, and does it appear to be sustainable?

The approach taken by the VAIE project is to:

- Identify candidate projects
- Develop an understanding of what these projects are doing with regard to faculty involvement

- Examine the outcomes of the faculty involvement, as the projects mature, through site visits, interviews, review of project reports, and secondary analysis of data
- Determine whether the engagement of faculty yields a value-added to reform process at the K–12 level, and if so, what features or combination of features facilitates this contribution

A first task of this project was to develop a framework that could be used to describe the projects being studied. A framework was needed to ensure a consistent and systemic way of approaching the projects and describing the specific theories of change they were exploring. A logic model for the overall Math and Science Partnership program existed, but this program logic model did not quite assume the lens needed for the VAIE project, a lens that viewed activities and outcomes primarily from the vantage point of work with higher education faculty, their role, and the results of their role. Although other ways of developing such a framework were possible, project leadership decided to try using a logic model for this purpose. Figure 11.1 presents the logic model that was developed.

Starting from long-term goals, staff brainstormed the range of outcomes that could be expected to result from such faculty involvement. Interestingly, although the main focus of the study was value-added to the K–12 educational system, the resultant list touched on changes at both the K–12 and higher education levels; the number of possible benefits offered at the two levels were about equal, reflecting a belief—or perhaps a hope—that faculty involvement could reap benefits across the K–20 educational system. As one worked backwards, this expectation that both the K–12 and higher education systems could benefit from faculty collaboration led to a logic model composed of a variety of short-term outcomes and related activities that reflected potential actions and benefits along the K–20 educational spectrum. This changed the focus of the study somewhat, broadening it to look at benefits for both partners.

As we have discussed previously with more traditional uses of the logic model, this model also constitutes a scaffolding for the kinds of data the VAIE needs to collect. For example, interactions between IHE faculty and K–12 science or mathematics teachers

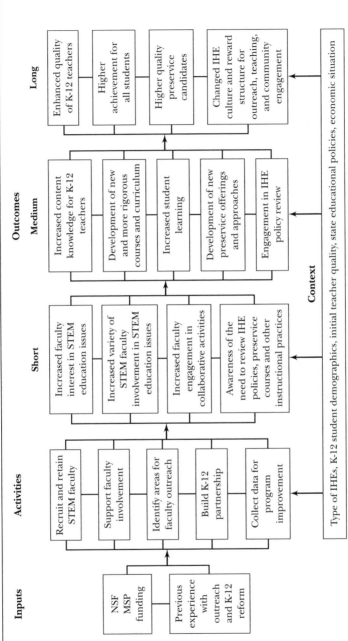

FIGURE 11.1. VAIE LOGIC MODEL.

Inputs

NSF MSP funding

Previous experience with outreach and K-12 reform

Activities

Recruit and retain STEM faculty

Support faculty involvement

Identify areas for faculty outreach

Build K-12 partnership

Collect data for program improvement

Outcomes

Short

Increased faculty interest in STEM education issues

Increased variety of STEM faculty involvement in STEM education issues

Increased faculty engagement in collaborative activities

Awareness of the need to review IHE policies, preservice courses and other instructional practices

Medium

Increased content knowledge for K-12 teachers

Development of new and more rigorous courses and curriculum

Increased student learning

Development of new preservice offerings and approaches

Engagement in IHE policy review

Long

Enhanced quality of K-12 teachers

Higher achievement for all students

Higher quality preservice candidates

Changed IHE culture and reward structure for outreach, teaching, and community engagement

Context

Type of IHEs, K-12 student demographics, initial teacher quality, state educational policies, economic situation are a primary focus of description and analysis. The VAIE will profile the activities undertaken to provide in-service professional development, as well as activities whose aim is to enhance the curriculum.

The activity "support faculty involvement" suggests the need to examine a range of potential ways in which IHE involvement could be encouraged. They include release time, stipends, rewards, and other incentives. One of the questions the VAIE addresses is the supports that are being offered, how they change over time, and whether some supports appear to be more beneficial than others in bringing about desired change at either the K–12 or the IHE level.

Another activity box that also stimulates data-collection efforts relates to IHE policies and practices. The VAIE explores institutional policies regarding engagement in activities such as outreach or K–12 in-service, how they evolve, and whether formal policy changes influence the outcomes of the project.

Because this logic model is a framework and not a fully specified theory of change, the VAIE logic model in Figure 11.1 has linkages only between groups of components; the model does not contain arrows that link activities to specific short- and long-term outcomes. Rather, the model lays out the potential subcomponents that might be linked; the task of the VAIE project as stipulated in the previous paragraphs is to look at how the individual MSPs are making these linkages and what the results are of the linkages formed.

Initial study shows that the projects are using faculty in a number of ways and are emphasizing various parts of the generic model presented in Figure 11.1. Figure 11.2 presents the logic model for one such variation.

This is a K–12 partnership involving one major institution of higher education and three school districts. Improvement is sought in the teaching (and learning) in mathematics and science. A major goal of the partnership is to create capacity for sustained, improved instruction by forming a teacher leader cadre that can continue to support in-service activities after the project has ended. This partnership employs IHE faculty in a number of ways: in-service activities oriented toward enhancing teacher quality and forming a cadre of teacher leaders who can

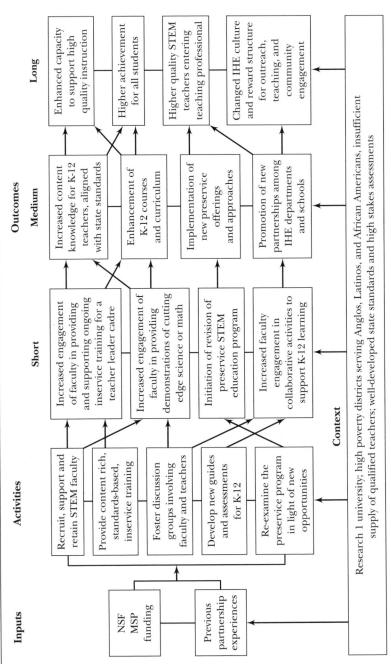

FIGURE 11.2. WESTERN STATE TEACHERS LEADER INITIATIVE.

sustain professional development, developing tools and materials to support the curriculum, and sharing knowledge and cutting-edge research through presentations and classroom visits.

A second major focus of attention is the IHE's own preservice program. This component includes not only changing the existing course structure but also forging closer relationships between disciplinary and education faculty at the IHE. Through this activity and others, the project also hopes to create new partnerships within its own structure and change the climate for outreach and teaching.

Figure 11.3 shows a logic model developed for another of the partnership projects engaged in the change process.

This second project focuses on improving the teaching of science at the high school level. In this project, the partners are several campuses of a university, a community college, and a research (nonteaching) institution. The specific focus of the project is to introduce more inquiry-based practices into the teaching of high school science. As the logic model shows, IHE faculty work with K–12 through curriculum development, interactions at workshops, and projects that engage them in collaborative efforts (both research and teaching). It is interesting that in this project IHE faculty play a relatively minor role in traditional in-service activities, delivering material at the workshops or summer institutes. Rather, the interaction here is through faculty-teacher collaboration of various kinds. Another unique feature of this MSP is the focus on changing instruction at the IHE level. Unlike many the MSPs we profile, where the IHE focus is on preservice preparation, this project seeks to change overall STEM instructional practices.

This VAIE is beginning its third year. To date the logic model has proven useful for organizing, synthesizing, and presenting data about the partnership projects. The logic model has been a way of describing the various theories of change being explored and the distinctions among them. It is now time to address the question of outcomes, taking the descriptions of theories of change that have been constructed and tracing impact to the school, classroom, and institutional levels.

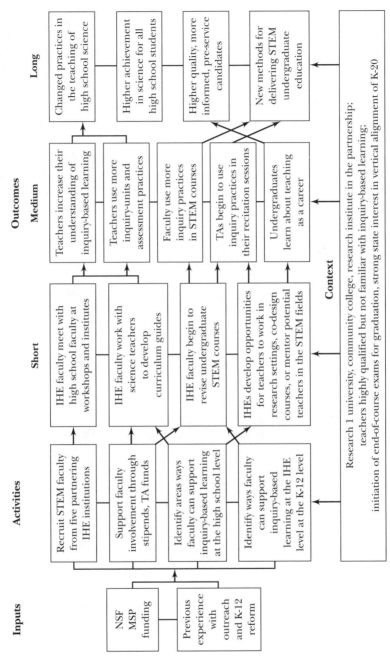

FIGURE 11.3. PROJECT VIM LOGIC MODEL.

Summary

This chapter illustrates another use for the logic model in evaluation and research: erecting a general framework for describing and exploring a family of projects with shared goals but differing foci and implementation strategies. It is the basis for identifying opportunities for data collection, serves as a starting point for developing individual project logic models, and offers a structure for comparing and contrasting strategies and their outcomes. The logic model is also a way of organizing a range of possible activities and outcomes into a single coherent structure, enhancing a project whose goal is to synthesize findings from complex investigations around a theme or themes of interest.

Questions to Consider

1. Using the logic models presented in this chapter, develop separate logic models for change in preservice instruction at the IHE level and teaching and learning at the K–12 level. What differences would you expect from treating these interventions as separate projects instead of having them integrated into one project?
2. Discuss the advantages and disadvantages of the two approaches.
3. Discuss the pros and cons of using logic models to study a family of projects. Suggest some other ways of approaching the task, and discuss comparative strengths and weaknesses.

CHAPTER TWELVE

USING THE LOGIC MODEL TO PROVIDE TECHNICAL ASSISTANCE

In this chapter, we discuss an additional way logic models can be used in complex projects to support analysis and improve evaluation. We also move outside the area of education and into community capacity-building projects to show how principles we have illustrated largely through examples in education and health apply equally well to other areas. Specifically, we discuss:

- Development of a logic model for evaluating an established community capacity-building program
- Modifying the features of the logic model to meet the needs of a particular program
- Application of this model as a technical assistance tool to improve project evaluation

BACKGROUND

The Appalachian Regional Commission (ARC) is a federal-state partnership that has operated since 1965 to promote economic and social development in the Appalachian Region. The example from ARC is based on work conducted by Westat and funded by the commission. Some changes to the logic model have been made in this chapter for illustrative purposes. A report on the study and its findings is at http://www.arc.gov/index.do?nodeId=57#eval.

ARC's Community Capacity-Building Program was reformulated in 2000 and enhanced to support two kinds of efforts: capacity building and telecommunications and information technology. A variety of funding strategies are used in the efforts, some centralized and others originating at the state or local level. According to Kleiner and others (2004), there is substantial variation among the funded projects; but generally speaking they can be classified into one or more of four program strategies:

1. *Vision and direction.* Strategic planning and regional or local needs assessments
2. *Involvement.* Small-scale projects that require the participation of community members in establishing or developing community organizations or associations; conducting outreach; and organizing meetings, conferences, or forums
3. *Skills and knowledge.* Group instructional activities, one-on-one instructional activities, and development of materials
4. *Support activities.* Furnishing or obtaining technical assistance

In 2003, ARC requested an evaluation that would measure program accomplishments and identify successful practices. In addition, ARC was interested in identifying how overall monitoring and project-based evaluation of performance could be enhanced. Cutting across these purposes was the broader goal of identifying a set of performance measures that could be used as a common metric to assess the projects. Because of limited funds, it was not possible to support a comprehensive, third-party evaluation. Rather, the idea was to build on data submitted by the projects themselves to develop a program-level assessment of success and set of recommendations for future evaluation activities.

BUILDING A LOGIC MODEL BACKWARDS

The investigators decided that one way of integrating findings from the hundred-some projects, which addressed community capacity building in a variety of ways, into a program-level analysis was to develop a logical model for the program and then superimpose the project-level data on the template. This use of the logic model at the program level was discussed in Chapter Two. In the present case, development of this model involved a bit of back-mapping, in that the program had been in place for a number of years and projects were under way. The challenge was to see if it was possible to create a logic model that would guide evaluation efforts accommodating most if not all of the existing investments. This does not mean that the logic model was driven exclusively by existing projects or that all parts of the resulting model needed to have a match in completed or ongoing work. Rather, the goal was to create an umbrella model that could inform assessment of current and future community capacity-building projects in the Appalachian region.

Construction of this model involved some steps slightly different from others we have discussed. Instead of developing the logic model primarily on the basis of the theory of change underlying the program, the staff used the program-solicitation and implicit model of change as one source of input. In addition, to get the bigger picture of the possibilities and ground the work as much as possible in the established research base, staff reviewed the literature on theoretical and applied perspectives on capacity building and factors that promote or hinder success. In addition, craft knowledge was obtained through review of applications and final reports to understand the purpose, scope, and accomplishments of the projects; discussions with program leadership in the Washington office and in the field; site visits to a sample of projects; and telephone interviews with an additional set of projects.

For the purposes of logic model development, these data sources amounted to a means of defining project activities, outputs, outcomes, and the measures used to determine them.

Figure 12.1 shows a logic model for the program. Again, we have eliminated the outputs to simplify the model.

The logic model contains:

- *Inputs.* The three basic sources of funding for the community capacity-building projects: Flex-E Grant Program, Appalachian Community Learning Project, and state and local funds.
- *Activities.* Because of the broad nature of the program, there is a considerable range of activities that could be undertaken.

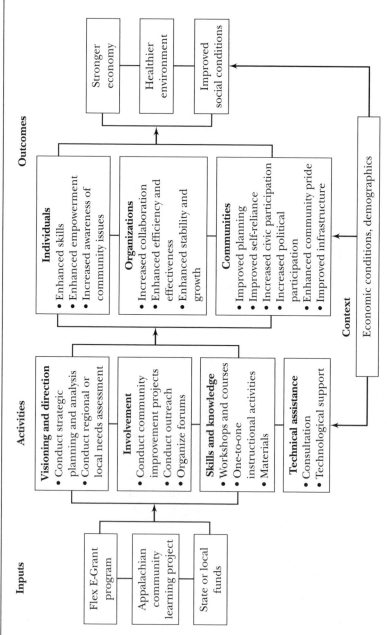

FIGURE 12.1. LOGIC MODEL MENU FOR ARC'S COMMUNITY CAPACITY PROJECTS.

Inputs

Flex E-Grant program

Appalachian community learning project

State or local funds

Activities

Visioning and direction
• Conduct strategic planning and analysis
• Conduct regional or local needs assessment

Involvement
• Conduct community improvement projects
• Conduct outreach
• Organize forums

Skills and knowledge
• Workshops and courses
• One-to-one instructional activities
• Materials

Technical assistance
• Consultation
• Technological support

Outcomes

Individuals
• Enhanced skills
• Enhanced empowerment
• Increased awareness of community issues

Organizations
• Increased collaboration
• Enhanced efficiency and effectiveness
• Enhanced stability and growth

Communities
• Improved planning
• Improved self-reliance
• Increased civic participation
• Increased political participation
• Enhanced community pride
• Improved infrastructure

Stronger economy

Healthier environment

Improved social conditions

Context

Economic conditions, demographics

Examination of the projects indicated, however, that activities could be grouped into four categories, each corresponding to one of the basic program strategies mentioned previously. For each strategy, some specific activities are suggested. They are illustrative only; many others could be added. For example, under the strategy of *skills and knowledge,* illustrative strategies include workshops and courses, one-to-one instructional activities, materials, and so on.

- *Outcomes.* This logic model presents outcomes in two ways. The first grouping of outcomes shows potential benefits for *types of beneficiary*: individuals, organizations, communities. As with the activities in this logic model, potential outcomes are used to illustrate what might be expected to occur as outcomes for each beneficiary group. The second group of outcomes classifies benefits not in terms of who is affected but in terms of the *aspect of the community or culture* affected—the economy, the environment, social conditions, and so forth. There is an expectation that the projects will have broader systemic impact extending beyond the confines of the particular set of activities supported through an ARC community capacity-building project.
- *Context.* Two broad categories of contextual factors are also specified: economic and demographic.

It should be noted that adding an outcome variable for aspects of the community or culture likely to be affected by the program raises some interesting challenges for the evaluator and for the program managers whose success will ultimately be examined in terms of the areas specified in the model. Two questions need to be considered. At what point is it legitimate to assess whether such systemic changes have occurred? Exactly what is it that should be measured to determine whether or not this outcome goal has been reached?

Take as an example the program strategy of enhancing skills and knowledge. If a project has a goal of increasing skills and knowledge in a particular area such as nutrition and the project succeeds with the community members who participate, what would be some legitimate indicators of a systemic impact? Is it that others in the community also gain similar skills and knowledge? Is it that there is continuation of demand for and access to increased skills and knowledge in the field of health and nutrition? Is it a change in understanding of the importance of continuing to expand education opportunities for the community's citizens? Obviously there is no one answer. Clearly, including such systemic impacts in a logic model should promote interesting discussion among the team members, even if the evaluation ultimately finds examination of such outcomes to be infeasible because of limited time or resources or because agreement on acceptable outcome indicators cannot be reached.

EXPANDING THE LOGIC MODEL

As the various sources of information about community capacity-building projects were explored, the investigators began to feel that contextual factors might play an important role in influencing the implementation and ultimate success of these projects. Rather than simply listing the broad categories of economic and demographic contextual variables, they identified specific attributes of communities that might be expected to enhance or pose challenges to project success—that is, assets and liabilities.

The site visits and interviews revealed that certain kinds of liabilities could have a significant impact:

- A local political system that communicated "negative norms" regarding the value of local decision making and community involvement
- Citizens who felt disempowered by previous failures
- Local corruption of various kinds
- Limited resources, whether material or nonmaterial
- Distrust and suspicion of outsiders

Assets identified included:

- Concerned citizens
- Availability of a strong leader
- Trust among workers in small, close-knit communities

Because of the importance of these variables in the cases examined, it was felt that they deserved greater attention in the logic model template as well as in project documentation. The logic model menu was amended slightly to call attention to the assets and liabilities as a critical part of the contextual variables (Figure 12.2).

Applying the Logic Model

The evaluators then applied the logic model to thirty of the funded projects to see what could be learned about the impact of the community capacity-building projects and their underlying theories of change. Two questions were asked: Could evidence be found of desired impact as predicted by the logic model? Did evidence exist in terms of hard data collected by the projects to show that the interventions undertaken relate to any outcomes found? In other words, is there reason to believe that the theory of change embodied in the logic model menu is accurate?

The results were mixed. In many cases, it appeared that antici-pated outcomes had in fact been achieved, but the evidentiary basis for these conclusions was weak and documentation of the theory of change poor. The evaluation concludes that "while many of the

FIGURE 12.2. LOGIC MODEL MENU FOR ARC's COMMUNITY CAPACITY PROJECTS
WITH ASSETS AND LIABILITIES.

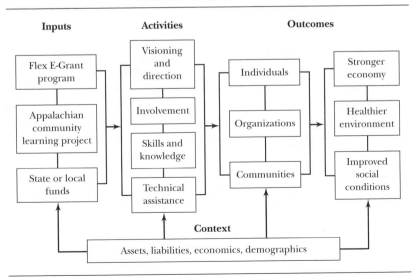

projects that we had examined had clearly contributed to community improvements, these contributions were rarely documented in a systematic manner" (Kleiner and others, 2004).

Three reasons were cited for this lack of documentation: inadequate delineation of long-term measurable outcomes with a concomitant focus on reporting of activities, insufficient evaluation expertise, and unwillingness to spend money on evaluation when managers knew "intuitively" that a positive impact would occur.

Not surprisingly, a significant limitation among the projects was failing to specify what success would look like. Most projects contained reasonable goal statements, but few established specifics on measurable outcome indicators and benchmarks for success. Returning to the example of the program strategy of increasing skills and knowledge, we find that projects frequently failed to specify how changes in skills and knowledge would be measured and what kinds of change were expected to occur. Were participants expected to know more facts? apply the facts to real-world challenges? use the new knowledge to impart leadership and support to others in the community?

Given this set of circumstances, it was decided to note the limitations of what could be concluded from the program evaluation and use the logic model in a technical-assistance mode to support the more consistent approach to performance assessment that the funders desired. Though the logic model was not accompanied by a full "how-to" manual, documentation gave guidance for things to think about in applying the model to a project and developing a strong performance assessment. Further, the logic model constituted a starting point for communication and discussion both among project staff and between project and program staff about evaluation expectations. By showcasing the logic model and accompanying report on its website, ARC also began to send a strong message as to what is required in an evaluation and the kind of thinking that needs to be undertaken to specify goals, outcomes, and benchmarks for success. A scaffolding has now been put in place that guides project evaluation and performance reporting, with the promise of enhancing accountability as well as what is learned from the various project investments.

Summary

This example illustrates how a logic model can function as a technical assistance tool as well as a framework for explicating the theory of change. It offers a way of profiling evaluation options that are clearly linked back to an underlying program theory. It shows how varying data sources—the literature, policy documents, and program plans—can be used together to create the logic model.

Questions to Consider

1. Development of the logic model used a variety of data sources drawn from the literature and back-mapping. Discuss the strengths and weaknesses of the various approaches for developing a logic model for a program that has been in place for several years.
2. The ARC logic model introduces a new set of contextual variables into the logic modeling processes: assets and liabilities. Do you find the addition of specifying these variables to be useful and important? Should specification of assets and liabilities be added to all logic models, or only certain project types?
3. The ARC logic model specifies systemic changes that are expected to occur as a result of community capacity-building investments. Do you find the addition of such outcomes to be useful? Are there situations in which specifying systemic outcomes would be counterproductive?

The Phases of an Evaluation

Whether they are summative or formative, evaluations can be thought of as having six phases:

1. Development of a conceptual model of the program and identification of key evaluation points
2. Development of evaluation questions and definition of measurable outcomes
3. Development of an evaluation design
4. Collection of data
5. Analysis of data
6. Provision of information to interested audiences

Getting started right can have a major impact on the progress and utility of the evaluation, and this book is devoted to the idea of getting started right. However, all six phases are critical to providing a high-quality product. If the information gathered is not perceived as valuable or useful (the wrong questions were asked), or it is not seen to be credible or convincing (the wrong techniques were used), or the report is presented too late or is not understandable (the teachable moment is past), then the evaluation will not be totally adequate.

This appendix is based on material presented in Frechtling, J. (ed.). *User Friendly Handbook for Project Evaluation.* Arlington, Va.: National Science Foundation, 1993.

DEVELOP A CONCEPTUAL MODEL OF THE PROJECT AND IDENTIFY KEY EVALUATION POINTS

Every proposed evaluation should start with a conceptual model to which the design is applied. This conceptual model can be used both to make sure that a common understanding about the project's structure, connections, and expected outcomes exists and to assist in focusing the evaluation design on the most critical program elements. There are many ways of developing conceptual frameworks. In this book, we suggest that the logic model is an ideal tool for accomplishing this stage.

Once this logic model is developed and connections are established, the next step is to review and clarify expectations for when the activities and impacts would be expected to emerge. Timing is part of logic model development, but it probably should be reviewed once a working model is established. As the evaluation process moves forward, determining expected time frames should entail revisiting decisions rather than assembling a set of new considerations.

DEVELOP EVALUATION QUESTIONS AND DEFINE MEASURABLE OUTCOMES

Development of evaluation questions builds on the conceptual model and consists of several steps:

1. Identifying key stakeholders and audiences
2. Formulating potential evaluation questions of interest to the stakeholders and audiences
3. Defining outcomes in measurable terms
4. Prioritizing and eliminating questions

It is obvious that program managers and the directors of individual projects are key stakeholders in any project, but it is important in developing the evaluation design to go beyond these individuals and consider other possible audiences and their needs for information. In all projects, multiple audiences exist.

The process of identifying potential informational needs usually results in many more questions than can be addressed in a single evaluation effort. This comprehensive look at potential questions, however, makes all of the possibilities explicit to the planners of the evaluation and allows them to make an informed choice among evaluation questions. As started earlier, each potential question should be considered for inclusion on the basis of certain criteria:

- The contribution of the information to the project's goals and the projects' local stakeholders
- Who would use the information
- Whether the answer to the question would yield information that is not now available
- Whether the information is important to a major group or several stakeholders
- Whether the information would be of continuing interest
- How the question can be translated into measurable terms
- How it would be possible to obtain the information, given financial and human resources

DEVELOP AN EVALUATION DESIGN

The next step is developing an evaluation design. Developing the design includes selecting a methodological approach and data collection instruments, and determining who will be studied and when.

SELECTING A METHODOLOGICAL APPROACH

In developing the design, two general methodological approaches—quantitative and qualitative—are frequently considered as alternatives. Aside from the obvious distinction between numbers (quantitative) and words (qualitative), the conventional wisdom among evaluators is that quantitative and qualitative methods have their own strengths, weaknesses, and requirements that affect evaluators' decisions about which are best suited for their purposes.

DETERMINING WHO WILL BE STUDIED AND WHEN

Developing a design also requires considering factors such as sampling, use of comparison groups, timing, sequencing, and frequency of data collection.

Sampling

Except in rare cases when a project is quite small and affects only a few participants and staff members, it is necessary to deal with a subset of sites or informants, for budgetary and managerial reasons. Sampling thus becomes an issue in developing an evaluation design. The approach to sampling is frequently influenced by the type of data collection method selected.

The preferred sampling methods for quantitative studies are those that enable evaluators to make generalizations from the sample to the universe (that is, all project participants, all sites, all parents). Random sampling is the appropriate method for this purpose. However, random sampling is not always possible.

The most common misconception about sampling is that large samples are the best way of obtaining accurate findings. It is true that larger samples reduce sampling error (the probability that if another sample of the same size were drawn, different results might be obtained), but sampling error is the smallest of the three components of error that affect the soundness of sample design. Two other errors—sample bias (primarily due to loss of sample units) and response bias (responses or observations that do not reflect "true" behavior, characteristics, or attitudes)—are much more likely to jeopardize the validity of findings. In planning allocation of resources, evaluators should give priority to procedures that reduce sample bias and response bias, rather than to selection of larger samples.

Comparison Groups

In project evaluation, especially summative evaluation, the objective is to determine whether or not a set of experiences or interventions result in a set of expected outcomes. The task is not only to show that the outcomes occurred but to make the case that the outcomes can be attributed to the intervention and not to some other factors. Ideally, in a true experiment representatives from the same population are randomly assigned to treatment or the control groups. Whenever this is not possible, other designs may be used, with a concomitant decrease in the perceived rigor of the work. Evaluators must determine how to handle this feature of the study design, determining what is feasible under the circumstances and what needs to be done for the work to be perceived as credible.

Timing, Sequencing, Frequency of Data Collection, and Cost

The evaluation questions and the analysis plan largely determine when data should be collected and how often various data collections should be scheduled. In mixed-method designs, if the findings of qualitative data collection affect the structuring of quantitative instruments (or vice versa) then proper sequencing is crucial. As a general rule, project evaluations are strongest when data are collected at two points in time as a minimum: before an innovation is first introduced, and after it has been in operation for a sufficient period of time. Studies looking at program sustainability need at least one additional point of evidence: data on the program after it has been established and initial funding is completed.

COLLECT DATA

Once the appropriate information-gathering techniques have been determined, the information must be gathered. Both technical and political issues need to be addressed. Keep a number of considerations in mind in planning data collection:

- Obtain necessary clearances and permission.
- Consider the needs and sensitivities of the respondents.
- Make sure your data collectors are adequately trained and will operate in an objective, unbiased manner.
- Obtain data from as many members of your sample as possible.
- Cause as little disruption to the ongoing effort as possible.

Even though all five of these considerations are important, two deserve some elaboration. The first is to recognize that before data are collected, the necessary clearances and permission must be obtained. Many groups, especially school systems, have a set of established procedures for gaining clearance to collect data on students, teachers, or projects. This may include identifying people to receive or review a copy of the report, restricting when data can be collected, and creating procedures to safeguard the privacy of students or teachers. It is important to find out what these procedures are and to address them as early as possible, preferably as part of the initial proposal development. In seeking cooperation, it is always helpful to offer information to the participants on what is learned, through personal feedback or a workshop in which findings can be discussed. If this is too time-consuming, a copy of the report or executive summary may well do. The main idea here is to create incentives for people or organizations to take the time to participate in your evaluation.

The second consideration is training data collectors. They must be carefully trained and supervised, especially where multiple data collectors are used. This training should include giving them information about the culture and rules of the community with which they will be interacting (especially if the community differs from that of the data collector) as well as technical skills. It is important that data collectors understand the idiom of those with whom they will be interacting so that two-way communication and understanding can be maximized.

The data collectors must be trained so that they all see things in the same way, ask the same questions, and use the same prompts. It is important to establish interrater reliability: when ratings or categorizations of data collectors for the same event are compared, an interrater reliability of 80 percent or more is desired. Periodic checks need to be conducted to make sure that well-trained data collectors do not "drift" away from prescribed procedures over time. Training sessions should include performing the actual task (extracting information from a database, conducting an interview, performing an observation), role playing (for interviews), and comparing records taken of the same event by different observers.

ANALYZE DATA

Once the data are collected, they must be analyzed and interpreted. The steps followed in preparing the data for analysis and interpretation differ with the type of data. Interpretation of qualitative data may in some cases be limited to descriptive narrative, but other qualitative data may lend themselves to systematic analysis through use of quantitative approaches such as thematic coding or content analysis. Analysis includes several steps:

1. Check the raw data and prepare them for analysis.
2. Conduct initial analysis on the basis of the evaluation plan.
3. Conduct additional analyses that are based on the initial results.
4. Integrate and synthesize findings.

Keep in mind that it is likely the initial analyses will raise as many questions as they answer. Starting from your initial analysis plan makes sense, but new opportunities are sure to emerge after the initial analyses are completed. Be prepared, therefore, to conduct a second set of analyses to address these further questions. Reanalysis cycles can go through several iterations as emerging patterns of data suggest other interesting avenues to explore. Sometimes the most intriguing of these results emerge from the data; they are ones that were not anticipated or looked for. In the end, it is a matter of balancing the time and money available against inquisitive spirit in deciding when the analysis task is completed.

DEVELOP REPORTS

The next stage of the evaluation is reporting what has been found. This requires pulling together the data collected, distilling the findings in light of the questions the evaluation was originally designed to address, and disseminating the findings.

Formal reports typically include six major sections:

1. Background
2. Evaluation study questions
3. Evaluation procedures

4. Data analysis
5. Findings
6. Conclusions (and recommendations)

Although we usually think about report writing as the last step in an evaluation study, a good deal of the work actually can and does take place before the project is completed. The background section, for example, can be based largely on the original evaluation design document. There may be some events that cause minor differences between the study as planned and the study as implemented, but the large majority of information—such as research background, the problem addressed, the stakeholders, and the project's goals—will remain essentially the same. Reports that are simply written technical documents are no longer acceptable; successful reporting involves giving careful thought to creating and presenting the information in ways that are accessible to a broad lay audience, as well as to professional audiences. Derivative, nontechnical summaries as well as electronic media are becoming increasingly important means of sharing information.

GLOSSARY

Accountability. The responsibility for justification of expenditures, decisions, or the results of one's own efforts.

Activities. The actions that are undertaken by the project to bring about desired ends.

Attrition. Loss of subjects from the defined sample during a study.

Back-mapping. Starting from the end of a process to develop steps leading to the desired outcome.

Baseline data. Facts about the condition or performance of individuals or a system prior to intervention.

Coaching. A supportive technique that involves working closely and collaboratively with a typically less experienced person to observe performance and provide assistance and feedback.

Collaborative learning. An approach to learning and problem solving that involves a team or multiple partners rather than a single individual.

Constructs. Themes or ideas. Major constructs are the central ideas on which a project or intervention is based.

Context. Describes the important features of the environment in which the project or intervention takes place.

Critical friend. An advisor or reviewer who offers constructive criticism supportively.

Cross-project analysis. An analysis that examines activities, results, or conclusions across multiple variations of the same program.

Design stage. The point at which a project, activity, or product is being conceived or planned.

Evaluability assessment. An examination of a project to determine whether or not it contains enough information for it to be evaluated in terms of its implementation or attainments.

Evaluation thinking. A way of thinking that emphasizes operational definition of critical components and specification of the kinds of data needed to measure success.

Explanatory evaluation. Evaluation that has as its objective assessing why something works (or does not work); it includes developing an understanding of the why and under what conditions in addition to examining whether or not goals have been achieved.

Formative evaluation. Evaluation that begins during project development and continues throughout the life of the project. Its purpose is to assess ongoing project activities and furnish information to monitor and improve the project. Formative evaluation includes implementation evaluation, which looks at how well a program is being implemented and whether it is being conducted as planned; and progress evaluation, which looks at how well a program is making progress in meeting its goals, including assessment of interim benchmarks.

Government Performance and Results Act (GPRA). Requires federal agencies to report annually on accomplishment of their funded efforts. This requirement includes establishing broad goals or strategic outcomes, performance outcomes, and performance indicators against which progress is assessed. GPRA goes beyond counting who is funded or who is served, placing the focus instead on results or impact of the federal investment.

Grain size. The level of detail on which an analysis is focused. Grain sizes may range from very broad to minute.

Impact. The intended or unintended change that occurs in a system, community, or organization that results from an intervention or a project.

Implementation. The act of carrying out or performing activities. Implementation can be characterized in terms of the extent to which it reflects what was intended in a plan.

Indicator. A measure that supplies information on the condition or status of a program feature; a factor, variable, or observation that is empirically connected to the criterion variable.

Inputs. The resources that are brought to a project. Typically, resources are defined in terms of funding sources or in-kind contributions.

Inquiry teaching practices. A teaching technique in which teachers create situations where students are to solve problems. Lessons are designed so that students make connections to previous knowledge, bring their own questions to learning, investigate to satisfy their own questions, and design ways to try out their ideas.

Key features. The most important or highest-priority components of a project, theory, or product.

Measurable. The extent to which the information provided offers adequate criteria for identifying a way of measuring and interpreting attainment of goals and objectives.

Meta-analysis. Combines the results of several studies that address a set of related research hypotheses.

Needs assessment. An examination conducted to determine gaps in knowledge, services, or resources.

Operationalizing. Defining in concrete rather than conceptual terms what is meant by a concept, goal, or outcome statement.

Outcomes. Changes that show movement toward achieving ultimate goals and objectives. Outcomes are desired accomplishments or changes.

Outputs. The immediate results of an action; they are services, events, and products that document implementation of an activity. Outputs are typically expressed in numbers or percentages.

Performance management. Managing by results; an approach to management that stresses the need to make decisions on the basis of the results of systematically administered performance measures.

Portfolios. A collection of work products of various kinds.

Product. A pedagogical process or material coming from research and development.

Program theory. A way of making explicit the assumptions underlying an intervention. It describes the causal linkages that are assumed to occur from project start to goal attainment and clearly defines the theory of change underlying a program or policy.

Qualitative evaluation. Approach to evaluation that is primarily descriptive and interpretive.

Quantitative evaluation. Approach to evaluation involving use of numerical measurement and data analysis employing statistical methods.

Reflective. The process of thinking deeply about an activity or process.

Response bias. Responses or observations that do not reflect "true" behavior, characteristics, or attitudes.

Rival definitions. Different interpretations offered for the same term.

Sample bias. Bias resulting primarily from loss of sample units.

Sampling error. The probability that if another sample of the same size were drawn, different results might be obtained.

Scaffolding. Supporting or providing a foundation for activities to take place.

Silo effect. The approach and result of thinking of things in isolation as opposed to looking at things as parts of a system.

Stakeholder. An individual who has credibility, power, or other capital invested in the project and thus can be held to be at some degree of risk.

STEM. Acronym for "science, technology, engineering, and mathematics."

Strategy. A systematic plan of action to reach stated goals.

Summative evaluation. Evaluation assessing a mature project's success in reaching its stated goals (also called outcome evaluation).

Systemic. An approach that takes into account all of the parts and the ways in which they interact and affect one another in service of reaching goals or end points.

Theory of change. Usually used synonymously with program theory; describes the causal linkages that are assumed to occur from project start to goal attainment.

Title I. Program established through the Elementary and Secondary Education Act of 1965. It provides funds to states, which in turn distribute funding to schools and school districts with a high percentage of students from low-income families. The purpose is to raise student achievement.

Treatment. New approach or intervention; whatever is being investigated; in particular, whatever is being applied or supplied to groups that is intended to distinguish them from other groups.

Umbrella model. A model or conceptual framework that is intended to cover a variety of components.

Value-added. Refers to the additional value created by incorporating a component or components. It is the residual effect of some manipulation.

SOURCES

Frechtling, J. (ed.). *User Friendly Handbook for Project Evaluation.* Arlington, Va.: National Science Foundation, 1993.

Scriven, M. *Evaluation Thesaurus* (4th ed.). Thousand Oaks, Calif.: Sage, 1991.

Wikipedia [http://en.wikipedia.org].

References

Callow-Heusser, C., Chapman, H., and Torres, R. *Evidence: An Essential Tool.* Prepared for National Science Foundation under grant EHR-0233382. Apr. 2005.

Connell, J., and Kubisch, A. "Applying a Theory of Change Approach to the Evaluation of Comprehensive Community Initiatives: Progress, Prospects, and Problems." In K. Anderson, A. Kubisch, and J. Connell (eds.), *New Approaches to Evaluating Community Initiatives.* Washington, D.C.: Aspen Institute, 1998.

Cook, T. "The False Choice Between Theory-Based Evaluation and Experimentation." In A. Petrosino, P. Rogers, T. Huebner, and T. Hacsi (eds.), *Program Theory in Evaluation: Challenges and Opportunities.* New Directions for Evaluation, no. 87. San Francisco: Jossey-Bass, 2000.

Huebner, T. "Theory-Based Evaluation: Gaining a Shared Understanding Between School Staff and Evaluators." In A. Petrosino, P. Rogers, T. Huebner, and T. Hacsi (eds.), *Program Theory in Evaluation: Challenges and Opportunities.* New Directions for Evaluation, no. 87. San Francisco: Jossey-Bass, 2000.

W. K. Kellogg Foundation. *Using Logic Models to Bring Together Planning, Evaluation, and Action: Logic Model Guide, 2000.* Battle Creek, Mich.: W. K. Kellogg Foundation, 2000.

W. K. Kellogg Foundation. *Logic Model Development Guide.* Battle Creek, Mich.: W. K. Kellogg Foundation, 2000.

Kleiner, B., and others. *The Evaluation of the Appalachian Regional Commission's Capacity-Building Projects.* Rockville, Md.: Westat, 2004.

Leonard, A., and Beer, S. *The Systems Perspective: Methods and Models for the Future.* Manuscript from the AC/UNU Millennium Project, 1994.

McLaughlin, J., and Jordan, G. "Using Logic Models." In J. Wholey, H. Hatry, and K. Newcomer (eds.), *Handbook of Practical Program Evaluation.* San Francisco: Jossey-Bass, 2004.

Rogers, P., Petrosino, A., Huebner, T., and Hacsi, T. "Program Theory Evaluation: Practice, Promise, and Problems." In A. Petrosino, P.

Rogers, T. Huebner, and T. Hacsi (eds.), *Program Theory in Evaluation: Challenges and Opportunities*. New Directions for Evaluation, no. 87. San Francisco; Jossey-Bass, 2000.

Stufflebeam, D. *Evaluation Models*. New Directions for Evaluation, no. 89. San Francisco: Jossey-Bass, 2001.

Uusikyla, P., and Valovirta, V. "Three Spheres of Performance Governance: Spanning the Boundaries from Single-Organisation Focus Towards a Partnership Network." Paper presented at Conference of the European Group of Public Administration, Ljubljana, Slovenia, Sept. 2004.

Weiss, C. H. "Nothing as Practical as a Good Theory." In J. Connell, A. Kubisch, L. B. Schorr, and C. H. Weiss (eds.), *New Approaches to Evaluating Community Initiatives*. New York: Aspen Institute, 1995.

Weiss, C. H. "Theory-Based Evaluation: Past, Present and Future." In D. J. Rog and D. Fournier (eds.), *Progress and Future Directions in Evaluation: Perspectives on Theory, Practice, and Methods*. New Directions for Evaluation, no. 76. San Francisco: Jossey-Bass, 1997.

Weiss, C. H. "Which Links in Which Theories Shall We Evaluate?" In A. Petrosino, P. Rogers, T. Huebner, and T. Hacsi (eds.), *Program Theory in Evaluation: Challenges and Opportunities*. New Directions for Evaluation, no. 87. San Francisco: Jossey-Bass, 2000.

Wholey, J. S. *Evaluation: Promise and Performance*. Washington D.C.: Urban Institute, 1979.

Wholey, J. S. *Evaluation and Effective Public Management*. New York: Little, Brown, 1983.

Wholey, J. S. "Clarifying Goals, Reporting Results." In D. J. Rog and D. Fournier (eds.), *Progress and Future Directions in Evaluation: Perspectives on Theory, Practice, and Methods*. New Directions for Evaluation, no. 76. San Francisco: Jossey-Bass, 1997.

INDEX